A
PRIVATE
Life

Growing Up Black In America

A
PRIVATE
Life

Growing Up Black In America

C H A S E   H A Y E S

ARPress
ILLUMINATING IDEAS
EMPOWERING VOICES

ARPress
45 Dan Road Suite 5
Canton MA 02021

Hotline: 1(888) 821-0229
Fax: 1(508) 545-7580

Ordering Information:
Quantity sales. Special discounts are available on quantity purchases by corporations, associations, and others. For details, contact the publisher at the address above.

Printed in the United States of America.

ISBN-13:   Softcover   979-8-89330-777-1
            eBook   979-8-89330-778-8

Library of Congress Control Number: 2024903986

A Private Life is about Civil Rights,
racism in America, and how the USC Trojans football team
beat Alabama in 1970 with an all-black starting backfield,
which ushered in the era of integrated college football in
the SEC and race-norming in the NFL.

{ Dedicated To Mom, Mike |

Mom was always close to me, almost like a big sister taking care of a little brother. There's always good and bad that you find in your parents, but they are blood, so what can you do? I had no choice but to accept my parents because that's what Granny Mary Scott's love firmly placed in me. I will always have that love for Mom because she's Mary Scott's daughter. It looks like Mike and I will have that blood running through an umbilical cord perpetually in cyberspace because of my book, so this is for you, Mom.

I also dedicate this book to my Uncle Carmen, who helped me in difficult times.

Contents

❴ Preface ❚

A Private Life is a memoir with a lot of mystery. I wrote the book for therapeutic closure to a life of blessings and curses, and because I never could figure out the magic I experienced as a child. A magic that protected me on my journey through life. I want the reader to share in some of the magic I experienced as a child from my magic peach tree, and a special monkey that stole peaches from that tree. His name was Joe Monday, and he was really a she. He (She) ate a lot of peaches from that tree, which I think gave her a lot of magic and the capacity to communicate with me. It's a wild ride through life with Joe Monday.

I was raised in a little French port city in the south, in Mobile, Alabama, where the last slave ship to America docked, the Clotilde.

The book will take you for a walk in my shoes in a life full of prejudice, bias, bigotry, inequity, and favoritism in the sixties and the early seventies, when black folks were looking to black politicians like John Conyers and the NAACP to rescue them from a world full of discrimination. I mean, it was so bad I thought I was living in a Mark Twain novel, so bad that I had to reappropriate the word "nigger." Right out of high school I enlisted in a Corps that was still living in the sixties. I can remember writing a letter to John Conyers. I'm still waiting for John Conyers to respond. I guess he was too busy chasing pussy to respond to my handwritten letter about what was going on up on Jackrabbit Hill, Camp Pendleton, California. Chasing pussy when a lot of young black Marines were being discriminated against in the Corps. He wasn't the only pussy chaser. I heard MLK was a rolling stone, too, back in those days. The NAACP was a bigger joke than Conyers' H.R. 40 bullshit bill.

The times have changed. We elected our first black president, who wasn't a pussy chaser, and a president after him who not only chased pussy but was a grabber, too. He's not shy. He told the world he was a pussy grabber and forced himself on women. His words were, "I moved on her like a bitch." White women voted for him knowing this. Voted for him after knowing that other women had spoken about how they had been violated. My journey may sound like a rant from time to time, but if you complete the journey with me and Mike, I'm sure you will forgive me for sounding like I'm ranting about experiences that seem incredible in this day and time. My mother, Mike, called me over the phone during some of my writing of A Private Life, so youwill hear me talking to her throughout the book. She made herself partof this journey.

I guess white folks probably think that now that they've help put a black man in the White House, we now live in a post-racial America, even though young black men are being gunned down by white police officers daily. Now that we have a real racist in the White House, I had to write my book over time, so there are jumps.

Most Pure Heart of Mary Church

Most Pure Heart of Mary Church is where I spent most of my childhood days serving mass as an altar boy. Father Oscar conducted the mass in Latin. If I was not in the Church or the classroom, I would be out on the football field with the Almighty Heart of Mary Lions practicing with the team. Most of the day was in the classroom. Mary Scott was still alive and was paying my tuition at Heart of Mary; she died last year there. I was ready to play football in my high school years at Heart of Mary, but the school closed down and I had to go to McGill-Toolen Catholic High School where my mother could not afford the tuition, so I had to do odd jobs around the school for tuition. There was no more football for me, something I was playing all my life. We lived in Granny's house. Granny paid my tuition, and then she was gone. Not only did I have to work at McGill, but I also had to work at the shipyard to support the family. I had to take Granny's spot because my paper route was not enough to feed the family. Daddy was making nowhere enough to feed my sisters and brothers, so I did whatever I had to do to put bread on the table; including borrowing a couple loaf every once in a while, from Carl's Grocery Store when it was delivered around 5AM in the morning, around the time I would be delivering papers in the neighborhood. My job was now to make it through McGill and take Granny's place as head of the household. Mom has had a few friends she was always introducing me to, and Dad was never there for any of my football games and whenever I saw him, he was drunk. He was an alcoholic who slave from sunup to sundown for FE Smith Electric Company.

Dad finally got a better job working for Clower Electric and they paid him fairly compared to what FE Smith was doing to him. My paper route with Mobile Press Register had more than 150 customers and I had to get the paper to each one of them before going to school every morning, which meant I had to get up every morning around 4AM to fold papers and get them on my bike and throw them. I got very sleepy in the mornings. Started building ships in the 9th grade, where I was put on a detail that was building the George Wallace Tunnel which started downtown Mobile and ran under the Mobile River emerging on Blakeley Island onto the Jubilee Parkway over Mobile Bay. I joined the AFL-CIO union at 15 and made enough money to pay some of my tuition over the summer breaks. I was 15 and all my siblings were younger than me except Tony, he was 17. Ricky was 14, Carol was 12, Earl was 9, and Tracey was 2. Granny spirit was with me and my imaginary friend in the sky was Joe Monday. Joe was an angel. Chico was one of many villains we had in the neighborhood, he was my girlfriend's sister boyfriend who had broken up with him and he did a drive-by shooting with his AR base machine gun. Joe threw me to the ground when he started shooting at everyone; one of the bullets hit Tiny's sister in the head. This kind of Black-on-Black crime in the neighborhood seems like a regular occurrence, with most of it being on Davis Avenue a.k.a. "The Drag" or now known as Martin Luther King Way.

After the Civil War and still today, white men's grievances are about the Civil War, State rights, slavery and voting. This was going on when I was a child and it's still going on in southern states today, doing everything that denies every man a vote. Even before the 1921 Tulsa Race Riot leveled the Black Wall Street Corridor in The Greenwood district, there was the Election of 1872 which was the most contentious in American history. After both parties complained of corruption, neither candidate would concede. Two governors claimed office and chaos erupted. Nope, not January 6. This shit happened after the Civil War. Politicians plotting to overthrow the government, and their supporters fought in the streets and attempted assassinations. The entire country watched in grim fascination as the wounds of the Civil War were ripped open and the promise of President Grant's Reconstruction faltered in the face of violent resistance and the birth of the Ku Klux Klan. The Colfax Massacre, in which at least 150 black men were killed by white supremacists.

The Supreme Court ruling that ended Reconstruction and became the foundation of Southern segregation, changing the American legal system for the next century. None of this was part of the history book I opened when I was in the 9th grade at McGill-Toolen Catholic High School. MLK Jr. was only dead for one year but should have made history. Martin Luther King Jr. was not mentioned except from the mouth of the history teacher who continues to label him a communist.

Brother Foster had my mother come to school to pick me up after the Woosley fight. Before she got there, he continued to tell me how "Black is Beautiful, but you are a piece of Brown shit". In just one week of high school, I encountered more hate than I did in all eight years at Heart of Mary. I was not going to tell Mike about what Brother Foster said because Granny wanted me to go to that school and I didn't want Mike to pull me out of there. I needed to find a way to take in all this hate and just get back home to my backyard which took me to another world.

We will never know the whole truth about Emmett Till's death, if I would have died in that pit at MCRD, no one would have known about me; I would have been lied about, like the Army lied about the Arizona warrior.

The 1966 Almighty Heart of Mary Lions (5th and 6th Graders)

We were the first black team to enter the CYO League.

First Row kneeling from left to right: Vicent Washington, Archie Shaw, Sam Battles, Marc Hendricks, John Thomas, and Lionel Alexander III. Second Row standing: Coach John Burke, Bruce Goode, Chase Hayes, Harold Pettaway, Elbridge Daffin, Ettienne Zak, Roderich Honer, and Rudolph Hayes. Top Row: William Burke, K.K. Perkins, Anthony Horner, Donald Perine, William Powell, Darrion Steinback, and Roderick Brown.

{ Introduction |

How did I go from being a poor black kid in Mobile, Alabama at a private Catholic school, picking up paper on campus after school each day to pay tuition, to making more money than the POTUS in 2007 with my own company, then back to being broke again after the crash of the economy in 2008? Well, it all started in Mobile, Alabama the summer after the assassinations of the first Catholic president and a nonviolent preacher. My grandmother, a mostly Creek Indian, also died that same year. Her daughter, Mike, was my mom.

Mike
A rare wildflower with a heart of gold.
A disputing mind that touched dad's soul.

Mike was a wildflower. Granny was my lighthouse. She kept me docked. I felt like a boat in a storm without granny. She left me with a wildflower for a mom. Mike had those sixties hippie ways. She would verbally abuse dad every Friday night because of his pay. After granny died, we were entrenched in poverty. That summer was the worst summer of my life. I had to go into survival mode. This old, World War II vet named Big Church took a bunch of us neighborhood boys to the graveyard to hunt possums. When we got to the graveyard, we jumped off of his truck to see how Big Church caught possums with only a baseball bat and an old metal milk crate. There were little trees over almost all of the graves, with possums sitting on the branches. They could barely move because they were so full from eating corpses from the graves. Big Church just walked up to one of the small trees and hit a possum in the head with the baseball bat, then grabbed it by the tail and threw it into the metal milk crate. After Big Church caught about three possums, we all began to jump on the truck to go home. The truck pulled off before I could jump on. I was running through the graveyard trying to catch up to the truck and hit a hill of dirt, falling into this grave with an open casket. I landed right on top of this old lady. Her scent got onto my body and I could not get rid of it. I had nightmares every night of this little old lady. I'd fall on her body and her eyes would open in my dream. I felt that I had awoken an evil spirit from her body, and it haunted me every night.

I took a trip to New Orleans to meet this Creole practicing Voodoo doctor called the Queen. I needed a lot of help if I was going to make it at this private school, which was known for its academic excellence. I told the voodoo doctor I didn't think I could make it any longer in this life. I told her I felt like I was going crazy. The past year I'd lost my granny, who'd meant everything to me. Losing Robert Kennedy, Martin Luther King "MLK," and my granny was too much for me to handle. MLK was assassinated that April.

April Dreams
That inward look into the mind,
where illusions dance in trifle time.

She lit up something that looked like tree branches and leaves and started blowing the smoke into my face, and did it for almost a whole hour. She also gave me something to drink that tasted stronger than moonshine and told me to return to see her next summer. I asked her as I left her house, "What was that stuff?"

She said, "Yage Ayahuasca."

I went to the park and could no longer smell the old lady, only the Ayahuasca the Voodoo doctor had blown up my nose for an hour.

xviii

New Orleans Voodoo is not Haitian Voodoo. New Orleans Voodoo is underground religious practices which originated from the traditions of the African diaspora with roots from the French, Creole, and Spanish, combined with this witch doctor's psychedelic brew shit.

When I got back home, I saw this little white monkey in our magic peach tree. I called him Joe Monday. He was a gift from Heaven, an angel. I think my great-grandmother, Leona "Nanny" Johnson, was reincarnated as Joe Monday. Which means he was really a she with a boy's name, "Joe," just like my mom had a boy's name, "Mike." Her sister also had a boy name, "Billy." Granny wanted all boys but had only one, Robert, and two girls, Mike and Billy.

Joe Monday helped me build my empire. The crash of the economy in 2008 destroyed it. I was an innocent little boy growing up in Mobile until Joe Monday came into my life. I thought that Yage must be some powerful shit to have me seeing this little white monkey angel. I call him an angel because he seemed to protect me from drive-by shootings in the hood, and just about all of the bad shit that was there in Mobile.

Mobile was part of the Dirty South back in the day, and I was a young, mischievous teen coming from the only Catholic grade school, Heart of Mary, which was in the ghetto. I then went to the only private

Catholic high school in Mobile, McGill Institute. I was young and so full of that Yage shit from New Orleans that it took Father O and all those crazy ass monks at Catholic high school to get me back in focus. The Josephite priests established the Catholic grade school in the early 1900s, and The Holy Ghost Sisters from San Antonio began the high school in 1917. The Dominican Sisters of the Congregation of the Most Holy Rosary from Sinsinawa, Wisconsin assumed operation of the high school in 1943, until it closed in 1968.

Growing up black in Alabama wasn't as racist as going into the Corps. Living through institutional racism is a bitch. I'm not my father, who was a selfless man, or my grandfather, who talked of killing a Confederate general. I could be a very angry black man if it weren't for those Dominican Sisters, the monks, the Josephite Priests, and Joe Monday. I also had a backyard that was so fucking amazing, it kept me preoccupied in my own little world. Pretending to be Tarzan, I'd swing from tree to tree with Joe Monday. I'd swim with moccasins and gators in the three-mile creek. The tree produced magical peaches, and those things took me to another world, away from the Civil Rights marches on Davis Avenue.

I guess having a short memory when it comes to something as abstract as racism and bigotry helps also, until you wake up one morning and we have a black president and politics from hell that compel nuns to buy birth control, not the nuns at the Heart of Mary. Their birth control was a wooden yardstick that they would use to bust your ass with.

Chapter One
Growing Up and Being Black in America

I'm sure Congressman Pretty Boy aka Rep. Paul Ryan, with the "misstated marathon times" and "the intense P90X workouts" was fortunate enough to experience some of the same teachings I received from the Dominican Sisters. Their roots are in Wisconsin. I just don't understand how a good Catholic boy like Pretty Boy got hooked on books like We the Living, The Fountainhead, and Atlas Shrugged. The Catholic teachings are the opposite of these militant, atheist books. He must also be a hermaphrodite. How in the hell does he know what's best for women's reproductive rights?

Congress and the Senate are full of UNDESIRABLES, a word I borrowed from the Corps. All recruits in the Corps were undesirables, niggers, and every other racist term that came out of Sgt. Gugle's mouth. All of these young Marines were scheduled to fight around the world, places like Niger in Northern Africa, where rich white boys never go in the name of freedom, then come back home to be called sons of bitches by their commander-in-chief. The last commander-in-chief who called people sons of bitches was my commander-in-chief, Richard Nixon.

The black Marines on Jackrabbit Hill had a name for me: "Songanzela." It meant "to guide." When they called me that name,

I thought about fucking Godzilla. Not because I was destructive or anything like that. It just sounded like they were saying "Godzilla," and it could have just been a head injury I had at MCRD. We had our share of dysfunctional undesirables in Mobile. Too many to save. The devil had the upper hand on God in the hood. The demons that needed to be exercised off the Drag back then was a mission impossible. The demons made the Josephite priests' mission to perform such an exorcism impossible, so they got out of that hell hole in 1968.

When I was around eight years old, the lady next door called me into her house while sitting on the toilet and gave me money to go get her some cigarettes and a loaf of bread. I guess exposing herself to me was her way of baptizing me into sex before Catholic grade school. I thought she had a raccoon between her legs. Good thing I didn't try to pet it.

There were a few black folks in the hood who were dysfunctional, to put it kindly. In my young eyes, it seemed as if everyone was promiscuous. Even dad. He used his FE Smith van to dick down Miss Frances. Most of the Civil Rights leaders back then were also rolling stones. The black men who were supposed to be setting examples for young black boys seemed to all be dreamers and womanizers. Joe Monday told me to forget about my dad because he was a drunk and a woman chaser, like all the black men I looked up to, even some of the priests in the Catholic Church. I guessed it depended on your gender whether promiscuity was considered good or bad.

I believe back then, black women teased young men to build studs, something that was passed down through slavery, like chitterlings. There seems to be a double standard. Women would be considered sluts if they were promiscuous. Sexual behavior in the black community really took on the meaning, "It takes a village to raise a child." You couldn't even go to the dentist without being violated by the only black dentist in the hood.

I graduated from grade school the last summer of innocence before going to another private school. Tony, my oldest brother, slipped some acid in my drink as we listened to the Creeper on the jukebox in "The Hole in the Wall," a hit house. I mean, fuck, Queen, the Voodoo doctor, fucked me up with her Yage, and now my own brother was slipping acid into a glass of wine. I noticed Joe Monday shaking his head no, but it was too late, I had already finished the shot from the glass. I was listening to the Creeper blasting his guitar, thinking I could fly like a crazy ass bird with no wings. That was a sick joke, sneaking acid in my drink. Tony and his friends thought it was fun to play these bullshit jokes on me. I was a little nerd to them because I was going to this private Catholic school that only families with means could attend. No one from my neighborhood had the money or the grades to go there. Tony and his friends were in the neighborhood high school, the hood public school, Central High.

Fossey didn't have to go all the way to Rwanda and Uganda to study Gorillas in the Mist according to my Cajun cousin Milton, he once told me Mobile, Alabama was Gorillas in the Mist. I took it as a racist joke being that he was on the Cajun side of the family, the part that came from the bayou of Southern Louisiana. Some of those Cajuns from the bayou think they are Caucasians, anything but niggers, the way they talk about niggers. Milton was mostly raise in a Catholic Boys Home and I can tell you personally myself, some of those Catholic Monks are some of the most racist S.O.B. that ever lived. I learn that my first year at a all boys Catholic private school from the principal, Brother Foster. When Brother Foster, first said something racist to me, I was in the 9th grade and felt attack. I did not know how to feel when Milton made that racist joke, like is this Cajun Nigger real or what. Mobile is where the last slave ship, the Clotilda, came to the United States, slaves was jumping off it when it pulled into the Mobile River, near 12 Mile Island, just North of the Mobile Bay delta. My great gran dna Nettie was a Native creek who was rapped by one of those FrenchCajuns down in the bayou, she must have been well over 100

When I last saw her right before Hurricane Besty came through. Down there under the humid heat, sex seem to take on some kind of jungle fever down there in that Gumbo melting pot of young people from Mobile to Lake Pontchartrain that was told to get out the house and go find a woman without telling you what to do when you find a woman at a young age knowing nothing about safe sex, my dad told me to stop hanging around my mother and get out the house and find my own woman, what kind of Gorilla jungle shit was that, I was about 12 years old at that time and knew nothing about girls, my dad had seven kids with my mom but felt free to dick down a neighbor every once in a while which I found more exciting then being wrong, thought it was all part of being a man in the jungle being that my dad was the only man I had to learn from. The only other man I look up to was MLK Jr. and back then everyone was talking about all the women he was dicking down, King having sex with a lot of beautiful women was a form of anxiety reduction for him, maybe my dad too.

I flew like a bird all the way to the Drag, the main vein of "The Camp Ground," Davis Avenue, aka MLK Way now. I stopped at the Dashiki club where "The Godfather of Funk" music was blasting into the streets. "Say it loud, I'm black and I'm proud." It was a summer of insanity, swimming in that damn Mobile three-mile creek with snakes and gators in the humid Alabama heat of the day, and watching preachers' homes and churches burn throughout the summer nights. Mobile, home of the real home run King, the Hammer.

I must have passed out, because the next thing I remember is being in my bed still tripping and Joe Monday playing with my ears with a feather, while my dog Rex watched Monday and barked. Between the barking and the tickling, I finally awoke from that strange acid trip. My friend and I were scheduled for mass with Father Oskar in the morning. If Father O didn't figure out that I came to school high, then those damn nuns noticed everything. The old tradition was alive with the nuns: spare the rod and spoil the child. The mass was done in Latin. If I didn't get my act together, there would be a price to pay.

I closed my eyes again and began to dream of Grand Bay, a family farm out in the country. At McGill Institute, I graduated under monks who could have easily been charged with assault and battery in today's society. Monks served on the faculty and were known as Brothers. Brother Cross Eyes was the Tell-Tale Heart Monk. Brother Foxy was a monk with the vulgarity of a drunken sailor in a Russian whore house. These two monks got my attention during my first week of school in the ninth grade.

My friend next door on Cuba Street was Big Baby, and I told him things about the ninth grade that I wouldn't tell my own mother. I was just fifteen, and Big Baby was sixteen. We started trying to manipulate his way onto a college football team in the Dirty South, the heart of Dixie, Alabama, and Mississippi. It was rumored throughout the neighborhood that the Bear had said blacks were not smart enough to play quarterback, and the welcome mat was not in front of the doors of the University of Alabama for blacks. This left a huge image in the minds of all blacks, as did the murders of those three Civil Rights workers in Mississippi. These things happened years ago, but still played a big part in the minds of blacks. I was too young to know why so much hate existed in the south back then, and still don't understand why it exists today.

I escaped to California, disregarding grandad's escape routes Post-Underground Railroad. I remember him saying black folks from Mississippi were jumping on trains headed to Chicago. Alabama trains ended in Detroit and the Carolinas went to New York.

I had four years of McGill and several more power meetings with Big Baby about his sports career before going anywhere. Our last meeting was when he was trying to make a choice for colleges to continue playing football. He was only one year ahead of me at the time. Our last meeting was at the last Mardi Gras Parade, the Order of Myths. He told me he was going to Texas Southern. I tried to tell him Alabama was a better choice because of what USC had done to Alabama with a black quarterback and predominant black team from southern Cal. They'd showed the Bear that blacks could play quarterback. USC had done more to integrate Alabama in sixty minutes that night than all the Civil Rights marches had done. Big Baby felt trying to compete against the White Hope out of Davidson high school for the job was impossible. He thought it would be too much with Alabama's history. Plus, the White Hope was an All American, too. Big Baby made the sports page every week playing quarterback, and I pretended to be his agent. I remember telling him back as a fourteen-year-old kid that even though the all- black college he was planning to attend was a Law School. Corporate America didn't go to black colleges to recruit lawyers. They went to Harvard. Back then the NFL did not give a lot of attention to all black colleges' football games. They sent scouts to Alabama games. Big Baby did not take my advice and went to his all-black college anyway, and he was not recruited.

I knew discrimination from a young age in life and wanted Big Baby to know that his chances of making it to the NFL out of an all-black college were limited. I wanted him to know that Corporate America was racist. It's a merry-go-round with how they recruit white athletic directors into all the major colleges in the SEC and other powerhouse divisions to this day. Alabama only integrated black football players after they were routed by USC in 1970. I thought Big Baby was strong enough to take whatever Alabama threw at him, including the White Hope. The White Hope was drafted by the New York Jets, and Big Baby was just another neighborhood legend. We had some black sports legends who made it big in sports and who came out of the hood in Mobile: The Satchel, Big Mac, Hammer, and The Wizard of Oz. Big Baby could have easily been one of these sports legends to come out of Mobile.

On my first day of high school, I was in a history class. I looked around and I was the only black person there. The history teacher walked over to me and said, "You have two strikes on you already: you are black and Catholic." There weren't too many laughs from the students. I guess the joke didn't go over that well with the kids, who probably were all Catholic. He went back to the front of the class and started telling us that MLK was a communist, instead of teaching us about MLK being a communist, he should have told us about the Tulsa Race Massacre of 1921, the four black girls that were killed in the Birmingham bombing or the Murders of Chaney, Goodman and Schwerner. I did not hear about the Black Wall Street until I was an old man and other Black Massacres in the South which I knew nothing about, I'm sure some form of CRT played a role in teaching back in the day. He reminded me of a character who had his own show on that Fox network that calls themselves a news network. On his show, he seemed to have an obsession with Obama, like my history teacher had an obsession with MLK. I was fifteen years old and just wondered why he was at our private Catholic school and not at a public school, where racial tension was a daily problem. Black kids were being bussed to all-white public schools from black neighborhoods in Mobile. I wanted to be at this Catholic school. I walked to school every day and stayed after school to pick up trash off campus just to be there.

The Maxwell House Coffee Can

After a summer of hustling copper, digging up antique bottles, my paper route, and working in the Prichard Zoo, that old Maxwell House Coffee can I used to store my money had close to $500 in it. I had just turned fifteen and the junkyard neighborhood mechanic, "Two Ten," had a little car I had wanted for months. He had promised to sell it to me when I was old enough to drive. It would almost break my bank to get it, but it was my only way to New Orleans. I had to get that old lady's spirit out of me and back into her casket. I talked Two Ten down to $200 for the car. Then I got an Alabama driver's license and bought a shotgun from Big Church because I feared traveling through Mississippi. Then I was off to New Orleans.

I told myself I wasn't going to let a police officer pull me over off the highway in the middle of the night in Mississippi. I did not want to become a strange fruit. I did not want to become the kind of strange fruit that was usually found in trees from 1882 to 1968, approximately3,444 pieces according to Tuskegee Institute. One hour into my trip, the Magnolia wilderness off the Fowl River began to feel like paradise.How could so much evil be in this land of paradise for as far as the eyecould see?

When I made it to the Louisiana state line, I began to see large plantations outside the city. I saw cotton being picked by mostly Creoles and blacks, and found my way into town. I found this little old lady who claimed to be the great-granddaughter of the Queen of Voodoo. Everyone called her "Queen." Her house had all kinds of strange bones and Voodoo dolls lying around everywhere. There was a picture of the Queen with a little white monkey on her lap in the front room of the house. The bones looked like the bones of small animals, like a dog and a monkey, and she also had a lot of Mardi Gras masks. It seemed like she blew Yage in my face for almost an hour and spoke in French. I finally left her place and walked around the French Quarter in a daze. Someone asked me if I wanted to visit the graveyard. I laughed and said, "No more graveyards for me." I ended up in Lake Pontchartrain where I met this beautiful Creole girl named Tiny French, and we got on the Zephyr together. She told me she was from Mobile, and I immediately forgot about all of my problems. Wasit Tiny French's beauty or just forbidden love?

Forbidden Love
My heart died a thousand times
for a beautiful nymph in whom I tried to confide.
It was forbidden love in a forbidden dream.
Though a cherished dream of love it seems.

Was it the Yage? That Zephyr scared the shit out of me, and probably scared that spirit out of me, too. I'm just happy it's gone.

Fishing for Blue Crabs and Lady Legs

I grabbed my fishing pole and crab net and jumped on my bike with Rex and Joe Monday running close behind trying to keep up. Then I stopped by the Orange Grove dump to dig up a few worms. I only went there to dig up worms so I could catch fish to put in my crab net, and then catch some blue crabs off the Mobile.

The antique bottle collector, this old lady, was at the dump, and she caught my attention. She usually paid you cash on the spot for bottles. Since she was there, I stuck around and dug for worms and bottles. I started digging in this one hole that was about seven feet deep. Someone had left it and I got lucky.

My first find was a purple ink bottle, which she bought for five bucks. A few minutes later I dug up a Hyde London Ink, which she bought for twenty bucks. What a good day! I had made twenty-five bucks. I was rich, and I had a bucket of worms, too. I was ready to go fishing, but I kept digging and came across a strange-looking lady leg bottle. It had Schroeder's Bitters, Louisville, and KY G W engraved on it. The old lady got really excited when I showed it to her and said, "I'll give you a hundred bucks for that Lady Leg."

Joe Monday was shaking his head no and Rex was barking at the old lady. Then she said, "A hundred and fifty bucks," and there was no way I was passing up a hundred and fifty bucks. I didn't care what Joe Monday and Rex thought.

I took the money, jumped on my bike, and went home, forgetting about going fishing. I was definitely rich now. A hundred and seventy-five bucks! I had a Maxwell House Coffee can that I kept my money in from my paper route, and it was hidden in a spot in our loft that no one could find. I only had a buffalo nickel left in that can, which was why I had to take those hundred and fifty bucks.

The word got around the following week that the old lady sold the Schroeder's Bitter bottle for $300. Well, turned out everybody did okay. The old lady made twice her money, and I was able to buy three pairs of Converse tennis shoes, a blue, white, and black pair, sweet low tops. I also got some shadow stripe pants and still had $75, and a buffalo nickel left in the Maxwell bank.

That antique Schroeder's Lady Leg was the most beautiful bottle I had ever seen, but now, I had $75 left burning a hole in that Maxwell can. I gave Joe Monday a little brown bag and told him to climb up the blackberry tree and pick some berries to make some more wine. I was running out of wine in the tree house. Then I took another $50 out of the can and went to the dentist's office to finish paying for some gold crowns (I'd had some gold crowns put on two of my teeth) and the rest was spent at the circus on cotton candy, candy apples, and getting on all the rides. There was nothing like the Zephyr in Lake Pontchartrain.

I had on some orange shadow stripe pants with white Converse tennis shoes and a Van Heusen white knit shirt to match my shoes. That's player's shit in the hood. I had to make a lot of money back then because I had a layaway account at several of the Jewish stores downtown. Only Jews sold top quality knits, silks, and Converses in all colors. I had a paper route, worked at the Prichard Zoo, and dug up antique bottles in between playing football, school, and being an altar boy and boy scout.

I had a pretty busy schedule in the eighth grade and had to retire my Tarzan act that summer. No longer was I swinging from tree to tree with Joe Monday on my back. I worked a lot that summer and had to really settle down and prepare for high school. I guess when you are having fun, time flies.

It had been just three years prior when I'd first seen Joe Monday. Hurricane Betsy had flooded the streets and our backyard with about four feet of water, and I saw Joe Monday swimming away from a gator with a moccasin in his mouth. He climbed up on top of the Hole-In-The-Wall, where he ate the moccasin while the gator swam around waiting for him or other critters to catch. I didn't know if that gator knew what he was about to get into, because I think Joe Monday would have ended up with some gator shoes. He was small, but if you've ever seen Tarzan fighting a gator, that's what it would look like.

I was going into high school and dad finally found time to take all the boys—me, Tony, and Ricky—to the Roxy Movie house, which was known as a white movie house because it wasn't on the Drag. I guess things are changing.

Dad did not like the Drag. He did not like anything that had anything to do with protesting. The Black Panthers film, Off the Pig, was playing all over the Drag. I never told him about Bobby speaking at Hope Chapel. He had no time for much of anything that had to do with protesting or unions. He worked hard, and drank even harder.

Joe Monday survived Betsy. She washed out what was left of a shack on the end of the property that had three separate units that Willie Scott's granddad built. Granddad always called me Little Chaser because I chased after him until he gave me a ride on his old Schwinn Bike that had a basket attached to the handlebars. I dropped the R on the end of Chaser and adopted Chase and his last name, Scott, to replace Robert Lee, the name my mother gave me. I have no idea why she thought I would keep the name of the Commander of the Confederate Army, who also owned a slave who was his cook from 1861 to 1865. I had the court decree my name was Chase Scott Hayes in 1990.

Nanny was this old, beautiful, dark Indian lady who never said a word the whole time I was in her presence. She had a long life, and was well over a hundred years old before Betsy came through. Mobile was an old French city on the Gulf Coast of Alabama, one of the best fortified cities in the Confederacy. The last slave ship to America, the Clotilde, came to Mobile in 1859. Union Forces took Fort Gaines on Dauphin Island within three days of the Battle of Mobile Bay.

Nanny was a beautiful woman with piercing eyes who was frozen in the past. She stared into space whenever I saw her. Her eyes told me she came back as Joe. Great Grandma Nanny had a very dark complexion. The complexion of Granny, her daughter Mary Scott, was almost white. I guess the stories Nanny knew were never told because she never talked.

The evacuation of Mobile began on April 10, 1865.
The Drag

Davis Avenue was better known as "The Drag." Every black ghetto has a Drag. Ours ran between our Heart of Mary grade school and the Booker T. Theater, where two of the longest miles of hell on earth existed, where I saw a beheading before there was a fucking Al-Qaeda. Where sometimes you had to dance with the devil just to get to school. The Drag has kept up with the black renaissance, and it's presently known as MLK Avenue out of respect to MLK.

White people seem to like to name some of the most destitute areas of cities to honor a King. How does a street named that way, usually marking a ghetto, honor a King? If you want to give real honor to MLK, change Wall Street to MLK Street. Fuck destitute areas in the ghetto, areas that have been, for the most part, left behind with the dream. In 2012, unemployment for blacks was twice as bad as the national average. Blacks don't need street signs; black people need jobs. We spent a trillion dollars over the past ten years fighting bearded cavemen in Afghanistan, building their bridges and schools, while America is falling apart. Blacks are unemployed. Of course we rank low in education. Our country is falling apart. We are now trying to educate cavemen when our country is almost ranked down at the bottom with them.

I know MLK would say, "That's the humane thing to do." MLK's dream is a myth for the average black man in America, from the Drag to downtown Mobile, from back then to the present. The vestige of slavery was alive and well then and now. If for some reason I was planning a trip back south, I'm sure I would still be paranoid about traveling through Mississippi at night because of the history of that state. It was very easy to be delusional as a black man back then, and especially today, because it seems like black lives don't matter. There's no longer strange fruit hanging from trees. It's lying dead in the streets all across America.

Mississippi has a reputation for killing young black men, America has a reputation for killing young black men, and it is all about history. I prefer today rather than yesterday because politicians are out in the open about their feelings today. I guess looking back to when that history teacher labeled MLK as a communist back in the ninth grade is like calling this POTUS a socialist now. These white southern lawmakers have no respect for this president, to call him a liar in his first state of the union, to claim he's more a threat to America than Al-Qaeda, to show cartoons of him as less than a man: a monkey.

Politicians say what their constituents feel. People are more open with their racist rhetoric. In 2015, these kinds of racist attitudes were reality. No work and a Jim Crow justice system causes black people to be delusional. Politicians need to stop all the fear mongering. The Arizona Senator corrected the old white woman about calling Obama a Muslim terrorist.

Bring most of the troop's home. Invest in rebuilding America. She's old and falling apart. Now is not the time to plant seeds of hate in young minds. We need to invest in companies that are willing to invest in Americans with "On the Job" training programs available to everyone who is willing to work. Create a real infrastructure plan even if it means new drilling all over Alaska. I would dig up Alaska like I was digging for Bitter's Lady Leg bottles. Our railroads are a joke. I'm sure high-speed railroads would create jobs from San Diego to San Francisco, from Los Angeles to New York.

The American economy is a joke. Old white politicians don't care about the King dream. They don't really see the POTUS as the president. They see the POTUS as nothing more than another black face that's got into office by voters' fraud. A militant radical. An Islamic convert. I mean, just being black is still a joke to these old white politicians. This POTUS is nothing more than a 21st century Colored Comet. They would rather blow up this country's economy than see him be a successful president. They moved the debt ceiling eighteen times for Reagan, and seven times for Bush. They should man up and stand up, like the South Carolina lawmaker did in the State of the Union. Let their hatred flow, stand up, and be heard, or go back to wearing sheets and hoods in the middle of the night.

They succeeded in turning back the hands of time rather than moving the debt ceiling, like what was done for every white president in the past. They have reminded the world of the Old America. The POTUS is just another nigger to the Birthers, the Tea Party, and all those who want their country back. "Their Country." My Nanny is Native American. I see only white faces in the Tea Party, no Indians, and they are delusional. They have no clue about history, and surely not black history. They have all of these code words for calling the POTUS a nigger, like "*gangsta*" government. Day by day they are coming out of the closets of South Carolina, Kentucky, everywhere, letting their real feelings be known. He's been a liar, a boy, a militant. I have heard more old white politicians and the media network people make racist statements about this POTUS than I heard in my whole life growing up in Alabama.

Black people should be immune to the word "nigger." After the Corps, I was. All of that slavery shit is in the past. We are now at the point where we are desperate for only economic growth. There has been very little economic growth for black folks over the past twenty years. I guess the removing of old street and freeway signs and replacing them with MLK signs in the ghettos was supposed to be something to be proud of. I guess it's like putting a token black coach into a major football program in the SEC or Texas. When you look at the man, the dream, you begin to see why those young black students were cheering after the Juice verdict. It had nothing to do with the Juice and more to do with black people, the criminal justice system, and economics. I'm sure the jury was delusional, along with all those young folks. It has nothing to do with anything but a history that we cannot seem to get past, not on the streets of America and not in the courtrooms of America.

We have a Jim Crow legal system that carries on this vestige of slavery because it's ingrained into the soul of America. It's what this country knows best: degrading blacks. My first attack didn't come from my drill instructor in the Corps; it was from one of the monks at McGill Institute and the principal. A white kid shot spitballs at the back of my head throughout the whole class in ninth grade algebra. We got into a fight after school and the principal only got the white kid's side of the story in his office, then came out calling me names that were very degrading and vulgar. It was so bad I could not even repeat it to Mike. I can see why my cousin Larry transferred to a public school. He saw the fight.

Mike had to come to school to get me from the principal's office, and I just knew I was going to miss the first Mardi Gras parade, The

Crewe of Columbus, all because of this after-school fight. I didn't even get to present my side of what happened. If this was the way this Catholic institution was going to be, it was going to be a challenge to complete four years. I couldn't let Granny down.

During my first week of school, I was made an example of by one of the monks, Crazy Eyes Moore. I fell asleep in class during the reading of "The Tell-Tale Heart." I received three grand slams on my ass with a paddle as big as a slugger's bat, about an inch thick. Then there was this Nazi history teacher's comments about me being black and Catholic, then the fight. I mean, I was already staying after school picking up paper around campus in that Mormon suit in front of my friends, which was pressure enough. I don't know how I did it. I knew Mike was not going to let me go to the Crewe of Columbus. She did let me go to the Mystics of Time parade a couple of nights later, though.

I finished four years at McGill Institute and joined the Corps, sold to me as the new Hollywood Marines. I joined the Marines to get benefits, to further my education, and to travel the world. Well, the type of structure and world experience I got from the Corps would be no better than the experience I got from the Drag, Davis Avenue, aka MLK Way.

Joe Monday

Uncle Paul came down from New Orleans when Granny died. I overheard him talking to someone about this magical monkey. Those were the good old days. The world was different back then. All of the black people living on Cuba Street in Mobile back then were professionals: doctors, schoolteachers, business owners, and just hard-working people.

That place is a fucking war zone today. All of the homes were nice then, with nice lawns, and the streets were covered with pine trees, magnolia trees, chinaberry, pecan, and wild berry trees everywhere. Everything was green and beautiful and peaceful. The only thing I can remember bad about Cuba Street back then is Big Baby's mom cooking chitterlings. It stank up the whole block.

Most of my friends came from good Catholic families. We went from the only all-black Catholic grade school in the city to the only Catholic high school in Mobile. Mobile is different now. My last memory of Mobile was grabbing a baseball bat and chasing a thug away from my drunken dad, who was stumbling towards our front door. Mobile is at a point of no return. Young people need to enter into a social contract or Joe Monday needs to put a little monkey foot in their ass.

Mobile has really changed for the worse on Cuba Street. Life is different, and America is different. Things used to be so honest. Now it's all corrupt. Congress is also at a point of no return and should also enter into a social contract instead of some kind of tax contract with this Grover Nut. The Supreme Court is beginning to look like Congress. Everything is political. Bush vs Gore. Citizens divided. It looks like the Health Care Bill that the POTUS signed into law is going to make it. The Catholic Church stood for something when I was a child and became an altar boy, a good Catholic. Like every young Catholic boy, I fell in love with Notre Dame until USC came into the picture. It's been quite a ride.

I suggest that we buckle ourselves in, because the ride is going to get crazy. The world seems like it spins faster and faster each year. The faster it spins, people start to get a little dizzy like Justice Scarface, and his mind is boggled.

The Corps wasn't ready for a change after MLK and the black movement in the sixties. After all of this time, America wasn't ready for a black POTUS. I never saw this kind of hatred with any other president. It seems like we should be so much further advanced with civility after the Colored Comet and MLK.

Ricky is the last of the family down on the Cuba Street property. Where would we be today without Jack? He stood up to a lot of bullies, including those bullies down in Alabama. Mike once said, "Well, you know the governor had a lot of black nurses at his bedside in his final days and was very fond of them."

Yeah, it's funny how the tide turns. I was slapped around a lot growing up because I always wanted to hang out with Tony and his friends, who were a couple of years older than me. I took my lumps. The spitballs in the algebra class in the ninth grade were the final straw. I admire those who take a stand.

One day I said, "Mike, what do you think of Dirty Harry?"
"Harry who?"
"Dirty Harry, the democratic Senate majority leader."

Anyway, he took a stand like Obama. He stood up to a lot of bullies in the Senate and the House. He's become mad as hell. Dirty Harry is the "New Jack City" from the sixties. Like USC, Jack, and MLK. They stood up.

Hate is what this country was built on, so it's not going to go away overnight. When the GOP had their 2012 convention, you witnessed something you had not seen since republicans were democrats: real live bigot politicians. They all found a home in the Republican and Tea Party. By no means is this a black and white thing, even though the GOP tried to make it that in the last election. I saw bullies in the NAACP years ago. I see blacks in the GOP party today who vote party lines regardless of the issue.

I was glad the election was over. POTUS won a second term. It's

18

history now. It was the most racist experience to black people since the Colored Comet, just hearing some of the things being said about the first Black POTUS. I can finally pull myself away from cable now that it's over. Black people still have huge problems in America. I can only hope that my neighbor was only kidding about someone killing the POTUS. He's an older white man, and he feels that the POTUS is the reason for everything going wrong. It took a black man for them to forget about Bush. Well, I guess the POTUS can resume being the leader of the free world now. Many thanks to "The Boss," a supporter of POTUS. The Boss did a great job getting out the vote. He is as much responsible for that win as millions of other supporters. The King of Bain can go back to being a Vulture Capitalist, hiding his money. The Kid, a supporter of the King of Bain, can go back down south to Alabama and hunt doves with Chicken Jarvis.

Big Church

Big Church was a big giant of a man who had a hit house on Davis Avenue (the Drag). He was a nightclub bouncer who carried a large gun on his side, an old colt .44 and a horsewhip in his hand like he was a slave driver. He also did roofing and hustled scrap metals, iron, copper, brass, batteries, anything that sold. He sold shiny (White Lightning) moonshine from his hit house and had tables that hosted Tonk games. His patrons came over to gamble and drink moonshine. He would go possum hunting at the graveyard almost weekly. Everyone was afraid of the Big Church.

My little brother Ricky worked for him as a roofer. I warned him that I would pay him back for leaving me in that graveyard, causing me to fall into that open casket. So, one night Joe Monday and I went to the side of his house and stole all his copper. Joe Monday put his junkyard, rabid pit bulls under hypnosis while I took the copper. I sold the copper to help pay my way to New Orleans, the only way to get the dead lady smells off of me. He told Ricky, "Tell your little bandit brother that I know he stole my copper, because no one else is that crazy."

He was right. No one else was crazy enough to risk being shot by that colt .44 or being whipped with that horse whip like a slave. After stealing his copper, I stayed away long enough to let him cool down. I played it off like I didn't know what he was talking about.

He said, "You little bandit. You kept telling me you would get me back."

I just laughed and played it off while he gave me this wild stare. He sucked on a pickled pig foot and continued to stare. He'd gotten hustled by me and Joe Monday, and he didn't like it. He was usually the one doing the hustling. I got away with it this one time, and I would never cross Big Church again in a million years. You just don't get awaywith beating Big Church. I think he knew that if he had done anythingto me, he had to answer Mike. No one in the ghetto crossed Mike when it came to her kids. She had connections with George of the Jungle, a black rogue cigar smoking cop whom even Big Church feared.I had the trump card: Joe Monday.

Grand Bay

Dad loved going out to Grand Bay to see Great Grandma Omie. She called dad "Rudy" and would put both of her hands on my face and say, "Rudy, you got some handsome boys." Visiting Grand Bay and Grandma was the best time of our lives. We would beg Dad all winter to go to Grand Bay. It was midway between Alabama and the Mississippi state line, in the town of St. Elmo, Alabama, a few miles inland from the Mississippi Sound. Great Grandma Omie and Nanny were about the same age, but Grandma Omie could do everything. She wasn't in a rocking chair like Nanny. She was out in the pine and magnolia wilderness, out there in the fresh country air. Grandma lived to well over and hundred, and I think her longevity had a lot to do with the old water pump out in her yard.

We pumped cold mineral water from that pump, and it was as sweet as Kool-Aid. I'm sure most of that water came from the springs of Franklin Creek. Grand Bay was like heaven: pecan trees everywhere, and cotton, soybean, and watermelons were the main crops. It was good to get away from Mobile and just relax. Hurricane Betsy came ashore near Grand Isle, Louisiana, which was closer to Grand Bay, then Mobile, which made me worry a lot about Grandma. We had snakes and gators everywhere in Mobile. Joe Monday barely got away with his life from Betsy.

So I begged Daddy over and over to go and check on Grandma, not realizing that all the highways were under water. I had to make it over to Pecan Street to check on Nanny. I got my boy scout knife and was headed out the door when Mike stopped me. I wasn't afraid of a few moccasins and gators. We swam with them in the Three-Mile Creek. Mike told me it was too dangerous because live electric wires were down. She wouldn't let me go. I could only sit on the back porch and watch my new friend, Joe Monday, eat snakes and other critters from the water.

The next morning, we began to hear reports about the damage Betsy had done from South Florida to the Grand Isle. Louisiana had been almost completely destroyed. I heard about caskets floating in Caminada Bay. I thought about the beautiful springs of Franklin Creek. As soon as the water went down, we headed to Grand Bay, and the closer we got, the more we were concerned, because we saw ships on land and damage everywhere. We finally came to Grandma's little dirt road, and as we made our way back to her little house, it was still there covered under a few trees. Dad opened the door and she said, "Oh I'm so happy to see you, Rudy." Her big brown glassy eyes were a sight to see.

Even though she was alive, it was the last time I ever saw Grandma Omie or Grand Bay. She died right after we left. She stayed alive to see Rudy and his kids one last time. I was told Uncle Carmen built a home there after living in Los Angeles for years. I understood why. Grand Bay was always magic to me as a child, and I can see how it would be magic to anyone who knew about that little place out in the middle of the pine and magnolia wilderness.

The Calm Before the Storm

Years before, this young black preacher learned how to put his foot in his mouth. He marched with Kings, rabbis, monks, priests, nuns and the Black Panthers. He stood hand-in-hand with the Panthers and led the march, singing, "We shall overcome." The KKK was firebombing black churches, homes, and burning crosses. MLK was dead. Mike was very pregnant with Tracey. I was running around in my Heart of Mary uniform civil rights march like it was a Mardi Gras parade. I play back these days in my dreams, which usually start around April, a month that won't go away in my mind, mostly because of Martin.

It was just one big street party to me; one I couldn't attend for too long on the Drag because Mike would have come looking for me if I wasn't home from school at a certain time. I had to be up early to deliver my papers. The day of this march wasn't anything special from any of the others. It just seemed empty without the King. None of that stuff was that serious to me. I was too young. My paper route the next morning was serious. I had to fight through a storm that morning while the Black Panthers ate soup in Hope Chapel and slept in warm beds. I remember struggling to hold a sack of papers between my banana handlebars while blinding rain hit me in the face and hurricane- like wind lifted me off the street. Sometimes I felt safer in the air than on the street because the water was rising.

When the water rose, every snake around found its way to the street. It seemed like I was running over coiled snakes everywhere and being snapped at.

The Black Panthers had talked about a revolution at Hope Chapel the night before. Shit, they should've gone on my paper route with me. I had a revolution every time I threw my papers in a storm, fighting snakes and all kinds of critters running everywhere. Joe Monday couldeat only so many snakes.

Rex was fighting through the blinding rain with me. It was me and my soldiers, Rex and Joe Monday. Bobby's message was a little different from MLK's, but they both were trying to liberate the south. Bobby was my mother's age, and he was speaking at Hope Chapel. He was later charged with making speeches for the purpose of inciting and encouraging a riot. Bobby was impatient and dynamic and MLK was tolerant, non-violent, and very patient with the movement. MLK was my hero as a child, but when is enough, enough? After growing up in Alabama, I thought I was headed for a better life in the Marine Corps in sunny California as a Hollywood Marine.

Chapter Two
The United States Marines

Hollywood Marines." That was the recruiting sign outside the Marines Recruiting Office in Mobile, Alabama. What a joke. It got me in the Corps. I had more Hollywood in my backyard in Mobile. I shot varmints like Jed Clampett. I swung from tree to tree like Tarzan. Hollywood could have done some of their Tarzan movies in my backyard. I swam in creeks with gators and moccasins. Shit, I had a levitating monkey like The Wizard of Oz.

You had to be very careful around a levitating monkey. He would take a big bite out of your ass if you were not careful. I also had a magic peach tree. All the magic peaches in the world couldn't prepare me for the treatment I received at MCRD, Marine Corps Recruit Depot, in platoon 2115. MCRD couldn't prepare me for Jackrabbit Hill on Camp Pendleton. I was brainwashed to say nothing about what happened in platoon 2115, something about having honor. I felt the only thing I had left was honor. So I said nothing about the mistreatment to the Board for Correction of Naval Records for years. It wasn't until 2011 that I felt that the treatment of Arizona Warrior was like the old Corps. No honor. It took the Arizona Warrior to show me that the more things change, the more they stay the same.

Sgt. Gugle had PTSD and should have been cleared with a mental evaluation if the Corps was going to move forward with changes in the seventies. The Corps integrated new recruits with delusional Marines returning home from Vietnam. Sgt. Gugle was one of those Marines who had no business working with new recruits at that time. He was right out of Hitler's Dreams. He was the most racist man I ever crossed in my life. He was a psychotic, delusional predator, a destroyer of young men.

Mad Dog was the age of those U.S. Track stars who protested at the Summer Olympics in Mexico City, Tommy Smith and John Carlos, suspended from competition after giving the black power salute, a clenched fist raised high over the head. Young black men from the sixties were part of that black power movement. I was coming of age in the seventies and caught the backdraft from Sgt. Gugle and the black Marines who were part of that movement returning from Vietnam in the seventies to Jackrabbit Hill.

O.J. Simpson was in that same age group, and I feel he did so much damage to race relations with one selfish act. After his school, USC did so much to integrate Alabama football in 1970. On my way to be a Marine, this was my first time ever on a plane. Our flight landed in San Diego early that morning, and big white buses waited outside of Lindbergh Field Airport to take us directly to the MCRD. The last U.S. ground combat forces in Vietnam were withdrawn while I was in basic training. I knew from the moment Sgt. Gugle jumped on that bus shouting all kinds of insane shit about the Corps that it was going to be a long summer.

It started with a drowning in the swimming pool. We had to jump in the pool with all our combat gear on and wait for our body to float back to the top of the water. Black people are not good floaters or good swimmers. One Marine was struggling in the pool with all of that combat gear on and was drowning. I pulled off all of my gear and was going to go after him when Sgt. Gugle hollered, "Get your ass back, maggot."

I hollered, "God damn it, he's drowning!"

Sgt. Gugle hollered, "Shut the fuck up, Marine." A couple of minutes later, he floated to the top. Sgt. Gugle finally went in after him, pulled him out of the pool, and tried to give him CPR. It was too late. He was fucking dead.

I got a letter from home later that night about the first female FBI agents. One was a former U.S. Marine and the other was a fucking nun. I can see the nun being an FBI agent because they are smart and tough. Not a jarhead Marine, though.

The following morning as we marched to chow, I moved my head a little on a "right shoulder arms command," a command where you change your rifle from one shoulder to the other shoulder. For this slight movement I was ordered to go to the pits for bends and thrusts. Sgt. Gugle took my M-14 rifle and blindsided me in the head with the butt. I fell unconscious and blood poured from my head. As the sun set on the ocean to the west, it was still light, and I could feel the cold breeze creep in off the Pacific as I trembled in my blood in the mud, wondering how I got there. I played this back in my mind and kept coming up with scrambled events. I awoke the next morning in my bunk, having no idea how I got there. I had dried blood on my head and was still dazed when Sgt. Gugle ordered everyone to the marching field. I was on the marching field fading in and out of consciousness having no idea where the hell I was.

Platoon 2115

I heard Sgt. Gugle shout, "Ladies, we are not going to stop marching until Private Flowers can change step." I was ordered to kick Private

Flowers in the rear end each time he screwed up the drill.

Private Flowers could not get it right. After being forced to kick Private Flowers by Sgt. Gugle all day on the marching field, I was then made to carry him to his bunk with a bloody rear end. Later that night, Private 747 got up in the middle of the night in an attempt to escape MCRD, and ran across Lindbergh Airfield, where flights were landing every minute, it seemed. Platoon 2115 was in the wrong place and the wrong time for me and any other Marines who came in contact with Sgt. Gugle.

Platoon 2115 is now just a chapter in my life, a chapter in Flowers' life, a chapter in the life of many innocent boys who made their last stand at freaking MCRD, not in a war zone. Paying the ultimate sacrifice on the watch of Sgt. Gugle, a murdering, psychotic coward. The recruits who did make it out of Platoon 2115 were transferred to Jackrabbit Hill. You don't put new recruits with undesirable drug dealing Marines on Jackrabbit Hill.

Jackrabbit Hill was full of dope-smoking professional killers returning from Vietnam who should have had mental evaluations before being integrated back into the real world. Sgt. Gugle, Private Psycho, all Marines should have yearly exams for mental fitness. I know I saw three murders with my own eyes in the Corps. I was left for dead in a pit. Sgt. Gugle should have been the one with the BCD, not me. I had enough discipline to obey orders. There are thousands of cover-ups in the Corps that would make the Arizona Warrior's story look like what it was collateral damage that ended up being a messy cover-up. I'm talking about murder.

The Corps at MCRD should be known for its cowardly treatment of young recruits. I did nothing to deserve this type of assault, and neither did Private Flowers, Private 747, or the kid left to die in that MCRD pool. My best friend on Jackrabbit Hill was this white boy named John. We would usually go through our daily routine on the Hill with all the racist so-called Mau Maus and Klans. After being around drug-dealing Marines every day, it wasn't hard to wonder if some of this stuff would eventually take a toll on us.

On the Fourth of July, John and I jumped on a bus with some acid John had gotten from one of the drug dealers, then we headed out to Oceanside. We stopped by a liquor store and waited outside for an older Marine to buy us a pint of 151 rum and a fifth of Thunderbird wine, and then we headed to the beach with the rum, wine, and a small bag of potato chips. I took a couple of sips of the rum and John gave me a piece of something that looked like clear plastic. I asked him what it was. He said, "Windowpane. It will take care of that headache."

I asked, "Windowpane?"
"Yea, acid," he replied.
I asked, "What does it do?"

John said, "Make you forget you have a headache. Make you forget you are on Jackrabbit Hill."

I told you about buying this junk from those dealers. I took one piece and washed it down with a swallow of Thunderbird wine. I told him, "They probably sold you some junk."

He said, "Try one more piece."

I tried one more piece. John had taken two pieces, too. Every move he made; I saw traces of him like I was back on that Zephyr roller coaster in Lake Pontchartrain. Fireworks were exploding in the sky with traces that lasted forever. Looking at the small bag of potato chips, one chip was like a thousand. You ate one and the traces of one chip kept going in your mouth.

We made it back to the bus stop and I helped John sit down. He seemed knocked out. I thought I was riding Santa's sled with all of his reindeer into the stars all over the night sky. Snow was all over the ground. The bus driver hollered, "Jackrabbit Hill."

I helped John to his bunk, then I went to the head where I stared in the mirror all night washing my face with water because I thought I was melting like the wicked witch in
The Wizard of Oz.

Sgt. Johnson came in the barracks shouting, "Reveille, Reveille! Get up, gents! let's go!"

Everybody got up in front of their bunk except John. Sgt. Johnson turned him over. He was cold dead. I could not believe it. My best friend was dead. Dead from two pieces of windowpane acid, 151 rum, and thunderbird wine. I thought he would pull through, but he never did. I guess if I hadn't stayed up all night throwing water on my face, it could have just as easily been me, too. When I was unconscious in that pit, I had several things going for me. My granny took me on a never-ending story trip for the whole time that I laid unconscious. I also had that magic peach juice running through my veins. I saw a lot of Marines who didn't make it. I think I have someone looking out for me. If it's not the peaches I ate from the magic tree, then it had to be Joe Monday.

Two weeks of liberty before reporting to Jackrabbit Hill. After three months of MCRD, what more can I do to fuck up my life even worse? My first fuck up was joining the Marines. After boot camp, I was so brainwashed, I went to a tattoo parlor and got this fucking Marine Corps bulldog tattooed on my arm in downtown San Diego while getting totally fuck-faced. I left the parlor on Broadway and saw this pretty blonde chick standing in front of a theater.

She said, "Did you just get out of boot camp?"

I said, "Yes. I'm a fucking jarhead now," and showed off that stupid fucking Marine Corps bulldog tattoo.

She said, "I give Marines a discount on blowjobs."

I hadn't seen pussy in three months, so I said, "Where?"

She said, "Come over here," and went into a vacant theater alley.

I said, "Damn, you are a pretty bitch."

After we got into the alley, I started feeling on her body and figured out she was a fucking tranny.

I said, "Bitch, here's twenty dollars. Get the fuck away from me."

I jumped on the next Greyhound bus going to L.A., got off the bus in LA, and went into a theater downtown to watch a Bruce Lee flick. I went to take a piss before going into the movie. While pissing, I saw a man dead in the urinal. I said, "Fuck Bruce Lee," and called my Uncle Carmen to come pick me up.

The next day, I hooked up with one of my friends from boot camp, Harry Hippie. We went to a theater in Inglewood and had barely sat down to watch the movie when gang members started shouting, "CRIPS here, BLOODS here," then, "PIRU here."

I said, "Damn, Hippie we better get the fuck out of here."

We got up and about ten fucking PIRU gangsters were on our trail because we were in an area of Inglewood where a Blood gang had claim PIRU. We ran through people's backyards and jumped fences and did what we had to do to lose those gangsters without leading them back to my uncle's house. I told Hippie, "Fuck L.A. We better get back to base."

Civil Disobedience

Saigon was falling. The Hammer was breaking the great Babe Ruth's record, and I was on a military hop to Ft. Leavenworth that feltlike it was going to fall apart in midair. A couple of months earlier, I was playing football for the Corps, flying missions over Tricky Dick'ssummer home in San Clemente. My gold Buick electric deuce and a quarter were on ice while I prepared to do the next year as I had the prior year in the Corps: locked up.

I was released from the brig during football season. I ran fast and caught every ball thrown my way. They had to have me on the team. We had a record of 23-1 over two seasons. My nickname on the football field was "Bobby Rat," the head of the rat pack. The only one with football skills close to mine was "Compton's Bobby Jones."

Jones was from Compton where he once saw a guy rob an armored truck guard from horseback. Only Geronimo can pull off some shit like that. When I wasn't playing football, I was locked up in the brig. I got one year in Ft. Leavenworth for destroying government property in an NCO club on Jackrabbit Hill. A bunch of other petty charges was added for my civil disobedience. That was okay. I would have been stuck with some real time and charges if I hadn't gotten off of Jackrabbit Hill. I was already in the brig for refusing to go into the field with Burns. After talking to him about the shooting incident, there was no way I was working with him or anyone else in Echo Company on Jackrabbit Hill. Especially not in the field with Private Psycho with live rounds in his M-16.

I had a cell in the front of the brig, and I was awoken by the sound of shackles. I saw a friend, Pvt. Riverside, shackled to about seven other black Marines, and my first thought was slaves. I hollered from the cell, "What happened, Riverside?"

He just dropped his head and said, "I'll tell you when I get in. They have attempted murder charges on all of us."

I just dropped to my knees and said, "Thank you, God, for giving me the power to refuse that work detail with those Marines."

Those Marines no longer belonged in the Corps. I knew that sooner or later, something would happen, and I needed to get off of Jackrabbit Hill even if it meant going to Ft. Leavenworth on petty charges. Vandalizing that NCO club had finally done it. In my mind, I was discharged from the Corps the day I was assaulted in 2115. This just made it official.

After a year in Ft. Leavenworth, I saw that my commander-in-chief, Tricky Dick, was being pardoned by President Ford. I knew not to waste my time requesting a pardon from the base commander who said that I was "lucky to be in the Corps and not hanging from a tree in Alabama." I was just a naive Alabama country boy wanting to go to Vietnam and fight for my country. Instead, I found myself on Jackrabbit Hill with the Vietnam War basically over. But it was just the beginning for me.

Second Battalion, 5th Marines, 1st Marines Division was returning home from Vietnam, and they brought that war all the way home to Jackrabbit Hill with them. I never knew how racist people were until I was on the hill integrated into this unit coming back from Vietnam. This was raw racism. The Catholic nuns protected me from that kind of shit growing up as a child. The black Marines returning to Jackrabbit Hill told me that the Vietnamese told them to go home, this was not their war. I guess they treated blacks the same in Vietnam as they did in America in the sixties. That calamity on Jackrabbit Hill taught me that, "War is about old men talking and young men dying."

Conduct Unbecoming

I resented everything about the Corps, including my personal treatment and their attitude about blacks in the Corps and promotion. I carried that resentment around inside of me and it became my greatest enemy. I was awarded a Bad Conduct Discharge out of the Corps. What kind of kid wears a uniform to Catholic school for twelve years, wakes up every morning at 5:00 a.m. to work a paper route from the sixth grade through to the eighth grade, and serves mass as an altar boy each morning after the route? Then goes to school after mass and football practice after school and scout meetings after football practice? What kind of kid continues to wear a uniform to an all-boys Catholic school from ninth through twelfth grade and stays after school every day for four years picking up paper off campus to pay his own tuition?

It's the kind of kid who did not deserve the abuse and assaults he received in platoon 2115.

I'm pretty sure my past twelve years before entering the Corps showed that I had self-motivation, self-discipline, and a determination to succeed. From Platoon 2115, I was sent to Jackrabbit Hill to train with some Marines who had some real issues: race, drugs, and delusional problems. I was only in the Marines for three months before I was in the middle of this tug of war. Blacks were calling me "Songanzela", meaning "to guide." They wanted me to complain about promotions and an MLK holiday.

The Hill was so segregated that it erupted that Fourth of July. Fireworks were spreading over the sky and riots in the streets, and their guide, Songanzela, was with my best friend, a white boy named John. Having John for a friend was living the King dream. We talked a lot about Jackrabbit Hill and why the Corps would integrate new recruits into this environment. We wanted no part of any of it.

John overdosed that night.

I asked for a Request Mask and got as far as the base general only to find out why the Corps was locked in a time zone. The request was for fair promotions in the ranks, and I was basically told by General Two Star that I was lucky to be in the Corps and not hanging from a tree back in Alabama. There has not been an honorable general in the Corps since General Two Star. From General Two Star to commandant, all of them are corrupt, whore-chasing, racist scumbags. A Few Good Men, my ass.

Black Marines told me about some wicked shit they had to put up with on the battlefield, like not getting decorations, promotions, and duty assignments, as well as having to endure the racial insults, cross burnings, and the Confederate flags of their white comrades. These experiences made them come up with the slogan, "You watch my back and I watch yours." They created a handshake called the "Dap," then called themselves De Mau Maus. Blacks were more worried about being killed by whites than the Vietnamese.

When they came across Vietnamese on the battlefield, the Vietnamese would say, "Go home, black man. This is not your war."

I left the Corps with a Bad Conduct Discharge and a head injury I never got treatment for. I struggled through the Corps not knowing what I was doing due to the head injury, and I continued to struggle through college after the Corps, knowing there was something wrong with me, but I had no medical insurance to see a doctor after my discharge.

Delusional

The famous phrase, "If the glove doesn't fit, you must acquit," was the most outrageous oral argument I ever heard. JC had to know that jury nullification was the only way of getting OJ off with double murder.

He knew he was working with a mostly elderly black jury, which was the opposite make up of juries that had locked up blacks in American courts unfairly for years, and sent some to their death prior to DNA evidence. He also knew that all of the police abuse of black men in Los Angeles had galvanized the minority community.

His legal maneuvers were not popular, but he was in the right place at the right time with a mostly black jury that I feel was disillusioned with America, as most blacks are. I think that jury gave OJ a pass based solely on the unfairness of the criminal justice system against blacks over the years. They had an opportunity to send a message to America while the world was watching. I really don't think they gave a damn about OJ. OJ is a lucky S.O.B. Lucky that black folks like myself and that jury are tired of a Jim Crow system that treats blacks differently from white folks and almost everyone else.

I enlisted in the Corps to be all I could be. I damn sure didn't think the racist shit I escaped from in Alabama would exist in California. When I got out of the Corps, I felt paranoid from what I learned from Marines returning home from Vietnam. It was always in the back of my mind when I applied for a job. I needed to wait outside of that employer's office to see if someone else was given the same job I'd applied for. Why wasn't I considered if I had more experience? That was the case with NASSCO after I got out of the Corps. It was delusional of me to think that big companies with federal contracts to build Navy ships wouldn't discriminate, but they do. I talked to a ship fitter outside of the NASSCO employment office after he was hired, and I was not. I found out that I had more experience than him. I went back in and demanded to know why he was hired and I wasn't. They hired me on the spot.

I have no doubt that discrimination is still prevalent when

unemployment is still twice the national average when you compare blacks with whites, and that's just one statistic. When you look at the pure numbers, it's incredible. I guess you can call me delusional. There are delusional soldiers out there committing suicide every day.

Forgotten Soldier

I see homeless soldiers everywhere and wonder why our great country is rescuing nations around the world when they should be rescuing our soldiers right here at home. My experience with the Uniform Code of Justice was as segregated as the University of Alabama in the sixties. I don't personally know the Burns story, but I know we all had a story. Things are not much better today, but seriously, how did black men go to Vietnam to die for what they left behind in America in the sixties and still today? The GOP has a member who attended a KKK meeting, as did the Marines on Jackrabbit Hill. Why are soldiers still returning home today in body bags, amputated or with mental disorders? Why are there no jobs here when they have freed nations around the world to come home to no freedom? Returning home to where all of the jobs, Apple, IBM, GE, GM, and some of America's biggest corporations have more employees in other countries now. Where is the honor to the men who died for those corporations to build their brand in a free country?

I have seen the faces of thousands of very young soldiers on cable shows who have died for so-called freedom. I don't see the honor, respect, or freedom for those soldiers. A handful of senators added insult to injury by blocking the Veterans Jobs Corps Bill. It's sad. These senators co- authored the Veterans Jobs Corps Bill, then blocked it to play the same games a do-nothing 112 Congress has been playing since Obama was in office. Those senators should be ashamed to call themselves Americans while these veterans have been putting their lives on the line in and out of Iraq and Afghanistan for the past ten plus years for their freedom. I mean America has left all the Vietnam veterans behind.

This bill was a democratic bill based on a proposal for a one-billion-dollar program outlined by Obama during the State of the Union Address, but has been amended to include a number of Republican-sponsored provisions. These senators fell in line with the extreme Tea Party reps and a Kentucky statesman to block anything that this president did. This was to prevent him from getting a second term. The statesman from Kentucky blocked a bill that could have saved the lives of thousands of suicidal veterans. This is the same man the POTUS calls his friend.

There's an old negro saying that blacks try too hard to make friends with whites. I guess this is a good example of that. This old son of Dixie for the most part has done more damage to this commander-in-chief and his soldiers than any other senator. He even said black men get some kind of special handouts.

Chapter Three
It's a Small, Small World

Six degrees of separation refers to the idea that everyone is on average approximately six steps away from any other person on earth, so that a chain of "a friend of a friend" statement can be made, on average, to connect any two people in six steps or fewer. Well, that means I'm only two steps away from the Teflon President, Ronald Regan.

"Butch" of the Little Rascals claimed to be a good friend of Dutch. Besides watching Butch on the Little Rascals growing up as a kid, I became friends with him years ago out at Kobey's swap meet. He had a stand usually across from mine every week, selling his childhood signature photos as a little rascal. I talked with Butch whenever he came out to Kobey's. He wasn't a regular there like myself, but he came out enough so that I really got to know him. He was an old man by the time I met him, and had to sell his signature photos to survive. He usually had kind words to say about Dutch and how he cherished the Hollywood relationship.

I told Butch I admired the love story of the Teflon President, too, but did not care too much for his politics. Butch and I never talked that much about the Little Rascals, but we talked a great deal about the Teflon President. I told him Dutch was for state rights when the citizenry ideology needed leadership in southern states and South Africa, being that there was functional apartheid in the south in the sixties.

When we talked about Dutch, it was never about his movies. I joked with him about black people never getting an apology for slavery until Slick Willie came into office. That apology didn't count because we saw Slick Willie as the first black president. We thought Slick Willie was the closest thing that we would ever get to a black president. Slick Willie said Obama was the biggest fairy tale he'd ever seen. He's a fairy tale to black people, too.

Butch had just finished an interview with NBC when I met him for the first time. He and most of Hollywood felt and feel that Dutch was a good man. I agree. Dutch, like most men, was good at heart. I just felt that his politics were bad. He mentored people like Santo Rum, The Speaker, and the Minnesota Congresswoman with all his racist rhetoric, like "Strapping Young Bucks using food stamps to buy T-bone steaks. Welfare Queen."

Dutch's racist rhetoric was a fear tactic used to scare white voters with tales of blacks doing something wrong or being given handouts and reparations, when whites have always been the biggest recipients of welfare programs. This is an old trick of the Militant Atheist Russian, to turn the tables and cast themselves as victims. They did it with the Willie Horton ad, The Speaker did it with the Susan Smith case, and Romney did it with his welfare ad against Obama.

Blacks will always be degraded as something different, even if Obama is the POTUS. Rudy Giuliani even feels that Obama doesn't love America. He should have just said, "Blacks don't love America." This kind of racist shit has been going on since Obama was elected to office. I mean, what in the fuck is he talking about when he says, "He was not raised like you and me"?

39

Rudy, he's more American than you. He was raised by white grandparents. His grandfather was on the battlefield in Patton's Army and his grandmother was Rosie the Riveter. I'm guessing if his father was named Jor-El and was born on the planet Krypton, he would be more American. I've never seen this kind of behavior abroad. I felt relief just leaving America.

Paris, France; Le Relais de Venise

Even with my limited French, I felt love in this restaurant and felt ashamed to talk about America in 2002. The meal is the "Small, Small World". It was thin, perfectly fried potatoes and swordfish sauteed in butter and garlic and was very delicious. The French were not onlypassionate people; they were passionate about their food and pairing the right wine with each and every dish. Women passed by the window on the sidewalk as you ate in the eighth district, and they all looked likemodels on a catwalk.

I was in Piccadilly Circus the night before, and they knew I had to be from down south in the states. I got a kick out of telling them I was from a little French port city in the South: Mobile. They laughed and talked about my southern accent that night in the Brasserie Zedel. I love London, but the French food just tastes better to me, or maybe it was just the magic of the City of Love: Paris. From Paris to Russia with Love.

Breaking Bread with Igor.

The quickest way to a man's heart is his stomach. There was a dark side of Igor, which I had to figure out before he was back under Putin's command. So, I shared a bowl of collard greens and Spanish muffins with Igor Kornilov. I made sure his last meal with me would be like a last meal request from death row because I didn't know what he may have slipped and told the Citadel in his little Russian town about his visit to Southern California. Being a Marine, I know everyone goes through a debriefing, and with that in mind, I made deep fried Pacific rock fish in Louisiana batter with the collards and Spanish muffins and sweet potato pie made with enough Courvoisier to make him sleep through his long flight.

Handouts

This POTUS is Superman, as far as I'm concerned. Growing up in the South, I knew where these old white lawmakers would start making all kinds of white noise. I've been black all my life. I have no idea what this Kentucky senator is talking about when he states black men got some type of handouts. I wish someone would have shown me where they were. The closest thing I ever got to a handout from white people came from a little white monkey called Joe Monday, and it was more like a kick in the ass instead of a handout. This is a stereotype I hear all the time. I wonder which black men get handouts. Maybe that black man sitting on the Supreme Court. Not me. I did not even know that being black was a problem until I got to the ninth grade and this Nazi ass history teacher reminded me at that time that I had this "being black problem." None of the Catholic nuns or priests ever said anything about race at the Catholic grade school. The nuns and priests even participated with blacks in the Civil Rights marches on the Drag.

I guess things start to happen pretty fast after the ninth grade. You are no longer a child. The hatred is more overt. The principal made it even more of an issue than the Nazi history teacher. I have been reminded of it more than I care to remember. I can't ever remember getting any handouts. I can only remember being disadvantaged because my father wasn't paid fair wages. He worked for everything he got, and I worked for everything I ever got. No handouts for our family. The closet door is wide open.

I'm sure there's more ready to come out, shed their sheets and hoods, and join the firm of the Grand Dragon. Their racist views and lies have no place in today's world. They only create groups like the Tea Party out of fear mongering. Joe Monday should pay those boys a visit and just slap the hell out of them with that little monkey hand of his. When people use terms like "*gangsta* government," "first food stamp president," and "work habits," they are using coded words instead of just calling a spade a spade. Just say "nigger government" or "nigger president." JW from South Carolina forgot where he was when he called the president a liar. He thought he was at a Klan rally and just could not believe a black man had made it as the first black president. He should have stood up and called him a nigger. That's what they are doing when they use all these coded words. They must be really dumb. Why try to disguise your real feelings?

It's hard to believe some of the trash the media is covering these days. Let's take the debt ceiling. The media make statements like, "Bush spent so much money," but the POTUS spent twice that much. How stupid do you have to be not to understand that the cost alone of all those trillions of dollars that Bush created comes with an interest rate that the POTUS can't control? So no, the POTUS did not make a bad situation worse. He does have a chance to make it better like Slick Willie did, who created twenty-three million jobs compared to Sir George's three million.

This POTUS has the chance to do something great, too. He needs to continue to push his job bill. Like Nike says, "Just Do It". He has newly found credit in Libya now, so if he really wanted to make a splash, he could use that credit to really bring gas prices down now that Libya is in a position to do more business with the west. Finally, the cost of a barrel of oil is dropping. Now he needs to throw a monkey wrench into the games that Wall Street plays with the pumps. The POTUS should also push harder for high-speed rails from San Diego to San Francisco and from Los Angeles to New York.

Keep pushing for other infrastructure projects. Look at what happened in Japan with their nuclear plants. We could have experienced the same in Virginia. Virginia is just three hundred miles away from New York and the borders of Canada. Tear down those old nuclear traps and upgrade them to protect the citizens now.

I made the same suggestions about the CH-47 and the CH-53, but no one listened. Good people just continued to die. If someone personally knows the POTUS, give him a piece of my mind. Tell him to get on a flight to Libya or send Joe "Just Do It." You would think the older these guys, like The Trumpster, get that they would lose some of that hate. I guess not. It's too bad.

We should be uniting as a nation to bring jobs back home that have been sent overseas only for an economic advantage to Corporate America. It smells. Corporate America wants to destroy unions. That's why they are shipping jobs overseas and moving their headquarters to Texas. There's this huge economic divide beginning to take back shape. If they get away with it in Wisconsin and Ohio, then they have enough fool people to believe, like the Tea Party, that someone is getting handouts. Life is like fashion. Give it time and it usually comes back around full circle. The "Lost Generation" is a term used to refer to the generation that came of age during World War I. My reference is to a generation that came of age during the Iraq and Afghanistan wars, wars that President Obama had to adopt from President Bush, wars that have put this country in a severe downward spiral starting around 2008 when Obama took office.

If the American Jobs Act is not supported by this do-nothing Republican Congress that would rather defeat Obama than save this country, then Bin Laden has succeeded in not only bringing down the twin towers but bringing down America and destroying our way of life. This do-nothing Republican Congress reminds me of the racist

Goon Squads that ran through the Mardi Gras parades dressed like cops beating people with nightsticks. The Tea Party is full of cowards who operate like the Goon Squads. They hate it when people say they are racist, but the studies speak loud and clear (see Notre Dame's study on the Tea Party). The Tea Party's most noted national figures include Republican politicians such as Ron Paul, Sarah Palin, Dick Armey, Eric Cantor, and Michele Bachmann, with Paul described by some as the "intellectual godfather" of the movement.

I think the Tea Party leader, Mark William, set to work discrediting himself and his movement by calling Obama an "Indonesian Muslim turned Welfare Thug." So, it's more than just their racist signs; it's whatcomes out of their racist mouths. They are nothing more than a Goon Squad that threatens to blow up this country over the debt ceiling. Wall Street stood up to most of these racist goons and could not rein them in during debt ceiling fiasco. When you fight fire with fire, you sometimes get burnt.

These Goons want you to give up your rights to unionize and your rights under the 7th amendment to sue for Unfair Business Practices. We don't need Tort Reform. We need Trade Reform, Bank Reform, and Tax Reform. Taxpayers paid to develop General Electric's skills, and in return General Electric ships 20% of its jobs overseas. Taxpayers saved General Motors, and they are building plants in Mexico when they could be investing back in this country by opening new plants to develop cars of the future in California, a state that paid a great deal of those taxes that saved GM from bankruptcy. Corporate America has built its purse right here in America, and now it's shipping a lot of jobs overseas and blaming this move on a shaky economy and too much debt. It's shaky because of Corporate America's greed and wanting to grow fatter on cheap overseas labor. Bringing the debt down is keeping jobs here.

Small businesses cannot hire without demand, and the consumers cannot buy because small businesses cannot put out a product without loans that were supposed to have been made available by ARC loans and the SBA through banks. The taxpayer's money went to banks to create those ARC loans, but the banks used that money to pay off their CEOs and to shore up their balance sheets. It's bad enough that this lost generation has to walk in the shadow of 9/11. Why test their vulnerability with the hate spewing out of the mouths of some of these goons? George Wallace is gone. The sixties are gone. This is a new world and a new time, and there's no time for a Tea Party. Our nation is split, and if this do-nothing Republic Congress attitude existed during World War I, we would have lost that war and we would all be speaking with a British accent, or maybe French.

Politicians, Corporate America, and judges are on the take (Clarence Thomas) to protect a way of life, a way of life which is tailored for Wall Street. The black William Jefferson (not Clinton) had 90k in FBI marked bills in his freezer. Seems like Lady Justice has a different balancing act for politicians, those with money who write policies for corporations that are too big to fall.

Now, William Jefferson was in over his head. He was playing poker with the Big Boys, and they had a stacked deck. Politicians are mostly lawyers; that's the bad news. Most of them are ambulance chasing, backstabbing, racist sons of bitches. It's part of their Southern upbringing, like the GOP's House majority whip. The lawmaker from Louisiana is what he is: a racist. He said it himself. He said he's David Duke without the baggage. DJT was my Robin Hood before he became a racist. He talked about going after China for stealing billions by thumbing their noses at our intellectual property laws, which I will detail more in the Small Business section of A Private Life.

Strange Fruit

Granddad's plot to kill a Confederate general and taking down

45

strange fruit haunted him till the day he died. Private Psycho had just watched Lady Sings the Blues upon Jackrabbit Hill. There was strange fruit in that movie. I don't know if that's what set him off. He was already nuttier than a fruitcake to start with. Blowing that Marine's head off on the rifle range may have had nothing to do with strange fruit, just robbery. I mean, he did shoot at a fucking squirrel with an M-16 while I was feeding it bread, so he probably was just a fucking nut. I helped send him to Fort Leavenworth.

Many people don't
realize that Adolph Hitler learned his philosophy of White Supremacy from what the KKK was doing to blacks during and before the 1920s. Granddad's stories, combined with Mobile's history of African-based cultural practices, was enough to give me a lot of sleepless nights. Nanny scared the hell out of me with her conjurings. She would sit in that rocking chair on her front porch just staring into space, never saying a word. I played the staring game one time with Nanny. She levitated my ass right off her porch. That is why I think she came back as Joe Monday. He does that levitating shit, too. I really think she reincarnated through Joe Monday. Joe Monday and Nanny both had the same dark eyes. Joe Monday knew how to talk to you through telepathic communication. Another reason I think Nanny came back as Joe Monday is Nanny's daughter, Grandma.

Grandma started talking to the magic peach tree after Nanny died. It wasn't until Grandma died that I began to see Joe Monday in the peach tree. Maybe only one person can see an angel at a time. Now it's my time. Mike told me she never saw Joe Monday, which also makes a lot of sense to me because she and Nanny never got along. Nanny tried to make her give up her firstborn, Tony, to a white family because she thought Mike was too young to raise a kid.

I wonder if Granddad buried that strange fruit on the Cuba Street property. It would answer a lot of questions about a lot of strange things, because those boys weren't that old when they were hung. Granddad said they were young, mischievous teens. Maybe they dropped the pencils from the sky.

When I played marbles with Joe Monday, there would be shots from somewhere else besides Joe and me. I always wondered why, when I got into a popgun fight with Joe Monday, I would be hit with more China berries than can fire out of just Joe Monday's popgun. It seemed as if I was in a popgun fight with four Joe Mondays. I guess there were mischievous slaves all over who didn't want to leave the Cuba Street property. My garden seemed to be cared for when I knew I didn't do it. All of the fruit trees and the garden yielded magical fruits and vegetables. It had to be those boys. I was too busy with my paper route, school, football, and other things. The crops were magic. Life was magic.

Mike would laugh and tell me never to tell anyone about Joe Monday. I guess that anyone who died on the Cuba Street property felt at home, because so many good spirits found the place just fun to hang around, no pun intended. Now, if Granddad did bury those boys on the property, Nanny could have brought them back because her powers were twofold of any of those Voodoo witches in New Orleans. I feel that her roots go back to the Clotilde, the last slave ship to dock on Mobile Bay and the French Creole, which is a powerful combination. Those boys could have also been summoned by Willie Scott because his spirit also hung out at the property. Those boys were probably his friends.

That property had ghosts from both sides of my mother's grandparents, her mother's mother, Nanny. Willie Scott was her dad, son of Eugene and Christine, who started the Family Feud. Christine, being a mulatto, probably had her reasons for wanting General Lee dead. Her mother was probably one of his slaves. She was probably his daughter. Grandma just got mad when Willie Scott was telling me all of these stories. He and great-grandmother wanted no part of Robert E. Lee. Neither did I.

That strange fruit scene in Lady Sings the Blues was a powerful scene. It could have affected Private Psycho, as if he were back in the 1920s. He was already a mental case. It didn't take much to send him over the edge. I guess I will never know. Private Psycho is doing triple life in Fort Leavenworth.

Masquerading As Catholics

What was that religious apocalypse bullshit coming out of the mouths of Rick Santorum and Newt Gingrich? These haters are masquerading as Catholics. The Catholic Church I grew up with never had anyone in the Church who talked about racist shit like Santorum or Gingrich does. My ninth-grade history teacher was the only one who talked like these old boys. He was as much a Catholic as Newt and Rick: he wasn't, nor are these clowns.

The Church stands for nothing these days. If it did, it would have denounced these fools a long time ago. Newt and Santorum have said many things against what the Church really fought for many years ago. The Church used to have a backbone before they started protecting priests over little boys. I guess anyone can call themselves a Catholic these days.

Santorum comparing Obama to Hitler was my ninth-grade history teacher comparing King to Communism. Santorum is a racist. I knew this when he stated he did not want to give blacks other people's money. Rick and Newt were in the spotlight because they were running for office. They are not the only old white boys who feel this way. There are a lot of these closet haters out there trying to force Obama to say, "Radical Islamic terrorism" when it's no different from "Domestic Christian terrorism." House Majority Whip, Steve Scalise, Ron Paul, and Rand Paul cannot outrun history; it's catching up with them. It does not matter because it's who they are. I guess Santorum and Newt hooked their wagon to the Catholic Church because they can confess all of their hatred then continue to hate.

There's a dirtiness to the world that confession can't do a damn thing for. John F. Kennedy was a Catholic, and Rick Santorum is masquerading as one. No, Rick "We Are Not All Catholics," not even Catholics are all Catholics these days. I fell from grace with the Church years ago because everything is dirty, not just the Catholic Church.

The Reverend Billy Graham was known worldwide, and his son Franklin is dirty. Franklin makes time to talk more about politics these days than the Word. In particular, Obama's faith. Our constitution protects everyone's beliefs, so why does Franklin Graham think he has more power than the constitution? Just like all Catholics are not Catholics, Franklin Graham is not Billy Graham. Franklin Graham damn sure is not Jesus Christ. Jesus Christ chose Disciples. Franklin doesn't get to choose who is Christian. No mortal man gets that choice. Franklin is just another rich preacher who refuses to give up those riches to become a true Christian. That's the calling from Christ: give up everything. Franklin Graham is tied too deep into politics to give up anything. If Franklin gave up his riches, he wouldn't have had a private plane to fly Sarah Palin on her book tours when she was McCain's running mate.

Then you have your Ted Haggards everywhere, so it's not just the Catholic priests these days presenting themselves in sheep's clothing. Once the Fox trolls found out about the real Sanford shooter, their so-called fair and balanced news started back reporting that Benghazi bullshit. So, if Steve Scalise is somehow removed from office, he would have the perfect resume to be a troll over there at Fox. Joe Monday hates fucking trolls.

The Vestige of Slavery

We cannot get a job bill or much of anything else with this black POTUS in office. You have this Kentucky southern lawmaker and his trolls who want to see this president fail. Unfortunately, there's more inequality today than there was in MLK's day. America has issues. Fox's head troll, G. Barker, woke up one day while Obama has been in office and said, "I thought I was on The Planet of the Apes."

G. Barker is entitled to his racist rants, as is Pat Buchanan referring to the president as "Your Boy" and arguing with the Reverend on MSNBC. Advertisers will decide their fate. If people stop watching that so-called fair and balanced shit, they lose advertisers. That's how America works. That's Corporate America, which sometimes has nothing to do with skin color or apes. Their color is green, the color of dollars they make through ads. If they are losing viewers, then the Becks of the world will fade into the dark world of radio.

My personal concern is about so many politicians, like The Pauls, Scalise, and the Minnesota congresswoman, who need to go back to school and take a refresher course in history. These trolls were voted into office with ideas that prolong the vestige of slavery instead of letting it fade into the dark like Beck. I get the free market, but I don't get the free market at the expense of the taxpayer. I don't quite get it. We take American taxpayer money to bail out GM, who then opened up a new 650 million auto factory in Mexico instead of California. It's a free market and all, but American taxpayers' money is putting Mexico to work when unemployment in America is at an apex.

Bachmann is too busy stuffing her own pockets with government money from what she claims is a *"gangsta"* government instead of creating a jobs bill. Where is Joe Monday when you need him to slap this bitch with that little monkey hand? She doesn't want to put America back to work because unemployment would go down and

Obama would get another four years in the White House. Which means four more years of Obama, maybe another Supreme Court Judge, and the beginning of that arc bending towards justice. The Pauls, Scalise, Bachmann, McConnell, and too many more elected politicians' main objectives are to make sure this president, Barack Obama, is a one-term president, even if it means putting off a jobs bill that would put Americans back to work.

America, the most powerful country in the world, has been hijacked by a few rednecks and a Tea Party that knows as much about the constitution as Bachmann knows about history. She wants to be the president of the United States and knows as much about history as that Alaskan governor, which is nothing. She has not corrected the record of her claim that the founding fathers freed the slaves. Maybe she thinks she knows something about black history because she seems to constantly make claims about blacks and slavery. I guess if she were serious about being president, she would hire a historian to check out the facts before making racist statements about history and the government being a "*gangsta*" government. She's on the take with her husband's business dealings with this "*gangsta*" government.

She signed a pledge for presidential candidates that references various historical anecdotes to contextualize its principles. The very first point it makes, however, suggests the group didn't quite do all their history research. She basically signed a pledge that claimed that black kids were better off under slavery than they are today under the first black president. While the laws governing slavery varied from state to state, one point was consistent: slaves were property and could not be party to a contract, including a marriage contract. This meant that no slave unions were legally recognized, and even the Emancipation Proclamation did not change this. The 1860 District of Columbia's Slavery Code dictated that ministers shall not "join in marriage any negro whatsoever or mulatto slave with any white person." Sec. 56 on p. 19. Slave owners encouraged slaves to couple up (so as to reproduce free new slaves), and slaves certainly held religious marriage ceremonies, but those marriages had no legal validity. Owners had no obligation to respect them or even keep married couples together on the same plantation. Children born into slavery were the property of their master.

Bachmann is wrong again on history by signing this pledge. Is this the best person that Minnesota has to offer to congress? I can say the same about Rand Paul and Mitch McConnell. If these kinds of minds continue to find their way into office, we will be on The Planet of the Apes. The first black as the POTUS offends some of these racists so much that they would run them over, not throw them under the bus. They'd run over every out-of-work American to make sure he's a one-term president. He's not even fully black. Why don't they give his white side the benefit of doubt? I did so with my white wife, a beautiful white woman with a degree in anthropology. She was usually in the backyard meditating in a circle of exquisite crystals or reading Shirley MacLaine's book, "Out on a Limb". Only in La La land. She was really out on a limb, but so was Bush. He raised the debt ceiling more than seven times due to all the corporate welfare he extended the rich and wars he started. Obama tries to clean up Bush's mess and has to deal with a closet racist like "the Donald," a two-bit hustler. After six years as the POTUS, a bunch of closet racists have tried to break Obama by hanging onto the vestige of slavery, which has been uncivilized.

Legal Profiling

There hasn't been profiling in Alabama since Dad worked for F.E. Electric, but that changed with the new immigration bill. Dad broke a lot of those racist barriers down at F.E. Electric, where his wages were not equal to his skills. He preferred to drink rather than challenge his employer for fair compensation. Dad was the kind of person who was just happy to be working and providing for his family. I started working on the George Wallace Tunnel in the ninth grade. It was constructed in Mobile at the shipyards of the Alabama Dry Dock and Shipbuilding Company (ADDSCO). I worked under the Steel Workers Union as a kid. Dad was not in a union. F.E. Electric took advantage of him until he moved on to C. Electric.

As a kid, I saw discrimination more in terms of pay than anything else. Chief Kolender claimed that blacks were born to fit a description (suspect) that was meant to be profiled, fingerprinted, and mug shot, all violations of civil rights. I personally witnessed some of his work when I first pulled into town in my gold electric deuce and a quarter. Edward Lawson witnessed some of his work, too. Under his command, SDPD has quite a record with the "DWB" stops. Saggy P was another black man who was pulled over for no reason. The police started beating him for "answering back" to them, and he was only sixteen. He was being brutally beaten by two cops before he was able to pull one of the cop's guns out of its holster and fired in self-defense. A jury later found him not guilty.

When I was pulled over, they made me and my friends get out of the car and get on our knees on a freeway going into town, now known as MLK Freeway. We were suspected of robbing a bank. We were taken to the police station, fingerprinted, mug shots were taken, and then were released. They were only stopping us because we were black and new in San Diego, purely "DWB." It was a way to document young blacks they did not have a record of on file. It's just saying, "We are gathering evidence for when you do commit a crime." I wish I had brought my levitating monkey with me from Mobile. The police can't shoot Joe Monday because he's too fast and dodged bullets like Bruce Lee. Before you knew it, that little monkey was kicking your ass like Bruce Lee.

Now, the last thing I would want to do is turn Joe Monday lose on anyone, but my boys and I weren't doing anything but having fun, jamming to Will DeVaughn's, "Be Thankful for What You Got." We were singing, "Diggin the Scene with a Gangster Lean" when Chief Kolender's boys pulled us over at gunpoint.

I really don't even know why we use Marines anymore in wars. Drop some of those levitating monkeys off in Afghanistan and just wait a couple of weeks. Those monkeys are real fighters. If you were walking down the street with one, people got the hell out of the way. I took one to the antique bottle field with me when I was a kid, to protect againstsomeone trying to steal a really expensive bottle. The bottle field was an old dumping site and the usual bottles we dug out of that field went foraround $5 or $10, but every now and then we would dig up somethinglike an eighteenth-century Lady Leg that could reach values all the way up to $150. Trust me, you need your monkey with you when you geta bottle like that. Your monkey will see you get excited about a good bottle and immediately start to levitate.

Joe Monday was as strong as a bat out of hell. I don't know how long he had been eating those magic peaches, but if he had been eating them for years, that explains how he was able to levitate and fight like Bruce Lee. I call him Joe Monday after Alexander Mundy, who was a suave cat burglar. Joe Monday became really good friends with me and Rex.

Chapter Four
Obama Derangement Syndrome

This POTUS had no idea what he was up against becoming the first black president of the United States. He was profiled like every black man has been in this country. Most of the POTUS profiling came from "the Donald," a two-bit hustler. MLK was hated because he was black. The Colored Comet was hated because he was black.

Growing up in the Dirty South in the sixties prepared me for Obama Derangement Syndrome. Old white judges like the Kentucky senator Old Micky had only one priority: to get this dirty black man out of his clean White House. This had to be worse than seeing a black man with a white woman down in old Kentucky for him. I wonder how Old Micky is taking the Lena Ad, a young white girl comparing her first voting experience to losing her virginity to a black man. Her voting virginity. This ad had their whole extreme Christian racist party in an uproar. They need to wake up and get out of the sixties already. They need an extreme makeover starting with ex-magistrate, Judge Zimmie, who is a liar and a profiler like his son, Zimmie Jr.

Judge Zimmie has already poisoned his son's mind with hate. Now he's using "The Objectivist Movement" tactic to try to poison a jury pool for his son. He knows that making it political is the only way to defend his son. He knows that "Stand Your Ground Defense" is not going to work for his son. He's a Jim Crow Judge. Montana's U.S. District Chief Judge Red Bull, Judge JS, Old Micky, and Zimmie are like half of the Judges sitting on the Supreme Court. They have no honor and are all Jim Crow judges. They will defend any of their decisions based on their judicial philosophy, which boils down to being political.

Hate is the kind of stress that kills you quicker than AIDS. The sad thing about hate is that it sells. People love to hate. I was only a kid when MLK was murdered. I only read about The Colored Comet. Black people walk around with heavy souls. I can't begin to understand places like South Carolina, Mississippi, and Alabama, where you can still smell the vestige of slavery in the air, see it on their state flags, feel it in your soul.

MLK gave his life for civility. Jack started this civil movement and paved the way for MLK. He made it possible for Jessie. Jessie laid the foundation for the first black POTUS. Teddy carried him over the finish line. Now he's part of this exclusive all-white club of presidents. By doing so, he created Obama Derangement Syndrome.

No matter what he does for this country, some will never see it. They cannot see past black. These judges are in the same mindset as the House Majority Whip, one of the Grand Wizard boys, a white supremacist, not being able to see past black. He's the first president to be profiled in the State of the Union. It's the dirty south. I don't know if it will ever change. It's a hotbed of ignorance and bigotry down there. This ignorance and bigotry easily spilled over into the 112th Congress, which had a lot of new Tea Party-backed political novices.

On the night of the POTUS's inauguration, republican leaders plotted to do just what Old Micky had been saying since the POTUS took office, which was, "Nothing." Whatever the POTUS did, he did it without the 112th Congress. They divided this country and used "the Objectivist Movement" tactic to blame it on the POTUS.

The Revolution Was Televised

If POTUS was a De Mau Maus Revolutionary, then so was Songanzela and 65,889,660 voters. I was one of his voters. The only thing I know about the revolution is what Gil Scott-Heron sang on his 1970 album, Small Talk. Gil Scott-Heron said, "The Revolution Will Not Be Televised," but it was. It took place in America, not Kenya. The POTUS was an American Revolutionary and commander-in-chief who ran on progressive liberal values. It was televised on TV, the internet, and cable all over the world. The revolution got 65,889,660 people to the polls to vote for the POTUS and his progressive liberal values, which included health care reform. He got four more years and I lost the friendship of one older white man on the block. He thought the POTUS was the cause of all that's wrong with this country. I can guarantee that it doesn't matter what this black president does or doesn't do. Deranged people like Tony, an old white man in the neighborhood, think someone should pick up a gun and blow his brains out.

Guys like Tony are usually down south. They still spew hatred because that is what was in their upbringing. The Tea Party hate to be called racists, but they run around town with racist signs that show their hatred more than anything else. Their biggest claim is that they somehow lost their country, and they want their country back. From San Diego on the West Coast to Mobile down south, natives are the real landowners, from the Kumeyaay Indians in San Diego to the Creeks in Mobile where my Grannies roots are. So, if anyone lost their country, it's the Indians.

When Juan Cabrillo rolled up on these shores off Point Loma, it was mostly Mexicans and Natives here in San Diego. Now we have a migration of tropical squatters sunbathing on the beaches while the natives are mostly isolated in the deserts with the coyotes. Meanwhile, this Tea Party movement runs around with signs talking about losing their country.

With the Creek Indians of Alabama is where my Grannies roots began. I think she summoned Joe Monday to help out in this revolution from her grave. Health care reform was part of this revolution, and Granny is going to need more than Joe Monday, because health care insurance is a scam. Junk policies were designed to beat poor people. Insurance companies make millions off of people who are too dumb to realize that nothing from nothing still leaves nothing. It's time for Slick Willie to go find a hobby or just shut the fuck up about those junk policies. They are NOTHING. For Slick Willie to say, "The federal government should let them keep them," is like people getting health care from Queen down in New Orleans.

The Kumeyaay Indians had all the land here in San Diego before Juan Rodriguez Cabrillo anchored his ship off Point Loma in the mid-sixteenth century.

Sea of Darkness

Years on years of winds and sorrows, built the dark sea and all its harbors.
1492 set sail a master plan which stormed the Bahamas, then Native land.

I do know that most of the reservations are back in the mountains and desert parts of San Diego. I last visited some of those reservations with my ex-mother-in-law, Nettie, who was a descendant of the Cherokee tribe. Her plot of land was mostly rocks and a rotted foundation surrounded by wild cactus. If anyone should want their country back, it should be the real owners. They don't care about the

Indians, and like one rapper said, "Sir George doesn't care about black people."

I first heard that from Nettie. She said, "Take care of yourself, cause 'no one else cares'." I took that to mean, stand up for yourself because no one else will. No doctors, lawyers, or politicians really care. Not even the POTUS can help without the help of Congress. If the right people are not elected to Congress, then the POTUS can only do so much. People need to start demanding that their congressmen work with the POTUS to rebuild this country, including those bridges that are falling down all over this great country of ours.

Lawyers only care about how much money they can line their pockets with, and if that means throwing you under the health care insurance bus, then that's what they will do. We are re-living the antebellum years, where if you have any color at all to your complexion, you will be taken for granted. In other words, personhood has no real value for blacks. It's open season on us. If I sound like some racist, it's because I have seen too many Sanford killings. It's obvious to me after watching the first black president's term. I didn't need to see the POTUS's first term to know what we had in America and what we have now. The Alabama Governor was loud and clear about his feelings, when GW first ran for governor of Alabama, and he lost to a racist, JMP, who had the backing of the KKK. After that loss, his aide recalled GW saying, "Sig, you know why I lost that governor's race? I was outniggered by JWP, and I'll tell you here and now, I will never be outniggered again."

Welcome to America. These old boys smile in your face and shake your hand, and it's not worth a dime. I can't get over Bush wiping his hands on Slick Willie after touching a black man in Haiti. What's in a man's heart eventually shows one way or another.

The Do-Nothing Congress Bark

Congress has done nothing since the 89th Congress in 1965, which was one of the most productive Congresses. John Conyers, Jr. sat on that Congress. I remember writing to him about Jackrabbit Hill. I got no response from him or his office. He was on the enemies list of my commander-in-chief, "Tricky Dick," at that time, which is the only reason I can think for why he did not respond. I thought he would have some idea of what young blacks were experiencing, since he was in the Army himself at a time which had to be a lot worse. He represented Detroit, but I wrote him anyway because he seemed to be one of the trailblazers for civil rights. Mr. Conyers had an opportunity to shine a light on Jackrabbit Hill, but he did nothing. He introduced bill H.R. 40 in January 1989 for reparations for black folks, which he seemed to do in every new Congress. That bill will do as much for black folks as naming a street MLK. Where are the leaders? I guess they are all gone. Jack, Martin and Robert, all gone too soon.

America was desperate for a new leader when out of nowhere came this bad, bad man, minding his own business over at Harvard Law School, taking a leisurely walk, smoking a joint. His name was Barack Obama. Barack was at the apex of his high when an imaginary friend appeared in front of him and said, "Barack Hussein Obama, you are now a super negro. You will guide this country from the fires of hell to the promised land. Enjoy your herb for now. I will get back to you in about twenty years with all of the details."

Barack threw down the joint and swore not to smoke weed again. His imaginary friend came back to him as promised one night in the White House. He was surprised because he hadn't smoked weed for twenty years.

"I see, my son, you have come a long way, as I knew you would.

Your mission is to turn around the Auto Industry before the country goes into a free fall. Pass Health Care Reform, send some seals over to Abbottabad, Pakistan, and eliminate this Osama Bin Laden fellow. Topple that Mohammad Gaddafi dude, too. Add a couple of liberals to the Supreme Court and get a nuclear deal with Iran. Forget about Congress. You are on your own; they will do nothing. They are mostly carnival barkers, birthers, and haters, and they will underestimate your emotional intelligence. That's good, because your work has just begun. Let them bark. You have three years before passing the baton off to Hillary. That's their job to bark. They are privileged and are mostly from much-protected census-designated places with estate wineries and shit like that. They will do nothing to help you. They feel public office, especially the POTUS's office, is a white boy's only club. You took something from them. You have been judged by your demeanor most of your life, which makes your odds to that office impossible. They tried to make you the angry black man, but the angry black mandid not show up in your demeanor. You are not a product of slavery here in America. The angry black man is a product of generations traced back to slavery. Your dad came to America as a free black man.So let them bark."

These barkers never had any intention of working with this first black POTUS. Paul "Objectivist Tactic" Ryan used this tactic in a speech where he tried to accuse Obama of splitting the people and creating class warfare. Ayn Rand's particular genius has always been her ability to turn the narrative upside down based on a philosophical system called Objectivism, where rational egotism is supported, and ethical altruism is rejected. In politics, they condemned the initiation of force as immoral and opposed all forms of collectivism and statism instead of supporting laissez-faire capitalism, which they believe is the only social system that protects individual rights. This political idea has been influential among libertarians and conservatives. Paul Ryan is a fan of the militant atheist, Ayn Rand, founder of the Objectivism Movement. There's a movement in the Republican Party that believe people are corporations. Mitt Romney had a slip of the tongue because he knows very well that corporations have to operate under greed, meaning that the Free Market needs to foreclose on the 99% that they used to climb into that elite status. Marco "my family escaped Cuba in the middle of Fidel Castro's Revolutionary War in 1959, in the dark of the night, under machine gun fire in the middle of a hurricane" Rubio, FL, Saxby Chambliss, GA, Johnny Isakson, GA, Mike "Don't Crap on Me" Crapo, ID, Jim Risch, ID, Mike Kirk, IL, Richard Lugar, IN, Dan Coats, IN, Chuck Grassley, IW, Pat Roberts, KS, Jerry Moron, KS, Rand "I have the right to govern under Jim Crowe Laws" Paul, KY, Rob Portman, OH, Jim Inhofe, OK, Tom "of course blacks get handouts" Coburn, OK, Steve "David Duke Who" Scalise, whose life was saved by black security guards and it still was not a wake-up call for this racist, LA, Pat Toomey, PA, Lindsey Graham, SC, Jim "I'll fly my Confederate flag till I die" DeMint, SC, John Thune, SD, Bob Corker, TN, Kay Hutchison, TX, Orrin Hatch, UT, Mike Lee, UT, and Ron "Secret Society" Johnson, WI, are just a few of the barkers from the House, and the barkers from the Senate also need to visit the wizard of Oz and ask for a heart.

These obstructionists refuse to give you a job, so why give them a job? Mitch "Who, me? With Jack Abramoff" McConnell, KY, Jon Kyl, AZ, Lamar Alexander, TN, John Thune, SD, John Barrasso, WY, John Cornyn, TX, Richard "My dad was in the KKK, not me" Shelby, AL, Jeff Session, AL, John "No MLK holiday" McCain, AZ, Lisa "I'm with the GOP (God's Own Party)" Murkowski, AK, and Steve "Cantaloupe Calves" King, IW, are among the politicians who envy the idea of a black POTUS in the white house messing with the Supreme Court and the Jim Crow laws that have been a solid foundation of America since Columbus landed.

Dreaming the America Dream

The America Dream is being able to have equal opportunities from birth, which is still too far reaching for too many black Americans. If every black would have gotten their forty acres and a mule, we would not be talking about Bill H.R. 40. Instead of the forty acres and a mule, we got five thousand strange fruits hanging from 1880 to 1960, mostly down south. The Butler story was very inspirational. It could have been Bobby's story, Jesse's story, Huey's story. I can go on and on with OBAMA highlighting them all. The Dream was fifty years ago. Black unemployment has not changed since that march on Washington. It was twice that of whites in 1963, and it's twice that of whites today. Jim Crow laws are still the foundation of our criminal justice system.

The Supreme Court has taken away the voting rights, a right Clarence Thomas barely got when he was of voting age. The election of our first black POTUS should have been a celebration. What we got was the kind of racial rhetoric that had been put away in closets all over the south with the white sheets and hoods since that first march. This country has been weakened because of racism. We have a do-nothing Congress that won't pass any bill that Obama sends to Congress, which was based on a plan to make Obama a one-term president. It did not work, and they stayed with the plan after the people re-elected Obama. Why don't they see that if they don't work with this president, it weakens our national security, and that gives Putin's Russia the opportunity to do the same? If Congress refuses to work with this president, why should Putin or any other world leaders, who have deep ties in Syria, Iran, and other parts of the Middle East?

When 2nd Bat., 5th Mar., 1st Mar., Division returned home to Jackrabbit Hill from Vietnam, I got an ear full of why I should not have joined the Corps. I was also warned by my older brother when I told him I was joining the Corps. He couldn't stop me because he was

63

standing a post in Cuba at the time I joined. These Marines returning home from Vietnam knew how the black man was treated in the sixties. I thought all this racial shit would be over by the time I got out of high school. I finished high school, got into the Marine Corps, and these soldiers were more delusional than the south. I don't think we will ever get a jobs bill or any bill out of Congress as long as Obama is president. Obama got the world to see what black people have been seeing their whole life. These nuts in Washington today make Jesse Helms look like an altar boy.

Congress treated Obama like the Corps treated me. It's not just Congress who's full of these cowards. What happened to civility? This is the real America, where you don't have to be educated to be elected to office. You only need the vote of people who think like you. The Corps treated me really bad, to the point that I wondered if my name was "a nigger," and if I should try to get my forty acres and a mule on discharge.

The Washington Monopoly

This exclusive club of insiders is the only way to become a player in this entrenched corrupted game of Monopoly in Washington. Once these guys get into public office, the temptation to screw their constituents is too great to overcome. All three branches are on the take with this 112th Do-Nothing Congress taking the lead. Congress once had access to non-public information in the Stock Market. It's crony capitalism. It's business. It's corporate America. It's Washington.

Their constituents are on food stamps and losing their homes. They should spend the same amount of time fighting for the president's job bill as they spend on inside trading. They argue about taxes and argue with each other about poor kids working in the place of school janitors. When Newt said, "Poor kids don't have the good models of adults working at home," I took it personally. I worked as a janitor as a poor kid. My father worked every day of my life as a kid. His sister, Dorothy, worked all of her life as a professor at Brooklyn Tech. His brother, Carmen, did his graduate work at UCLA and worked all his life. My granny worked all of her life as a nurse at Paradise Hospital.

It's hard to believe that Newt is Catholic. There are not a lot of Catholics who say the racist shit I hear coming out of his mouth. To question a poor kid's work ethic is part of his demeanor. Maybe Newt is one of those Catholics Michael Moore wrote about in Here Comes Trouble who cheered at the announcement of King's assassination. I wouldn't believe that in a million years, Catholics cheering the announcement of King's assassination.

Well, it didn't take a million years. It only took until August 24, 2012, when Mitt Romney supposedly made a birther joke about his birthplace, and I saw Catholic nuns cheering. Seven years ago, black people in New Orleans were dying and being called refugees after Katrina. Seven years later, jokes were still being made about the first black president's birth certificate. I don't see it as a joke, not when it comes from someone who belongs to a church that discriminated against blacks well after the Civil Rights Movement, someone who gives birthers like the Trumpster a role in their convention. I don't see a fucking thing funny.

I was that poor kid working after school while rich white kids were in study hall. I built ships in the summertime. I had a paper route in grade school and worked at the Prichard Zoo. Work ethic. Maybe this is the handout that Tom Coburn is referring to when he said black men got handouts. Newt has been saying racist crap for a long time now. Obama did not start this class war. It started on K Street years ago, and runs all over Capitol Hill. These are where the handouts are made. The reason jobs are being sent overseas has nothing to do with poor kids' work ethic. Politicians are being courted from day one by lobbyists for the day when they leave public life. It's institutional corruption. A revolving door.

I knew I couldn't go after the Marine Corps. It's part of the executive branch of government. The Pentagon is Boardwalk. The Warrior did a good job of showing how these cowards work. Politicians are the biggest Jekyll and Hyde whores I have ever seen. They will say anything to get elected, and usually, it's something to scare white folks, like Newt Gingrich blaming the democrats for SS's lie about black men kidnapping her kids. Tom Coburn lying about black men getting handouts. See where this theme is going?

Barack Obama is being blamed for all of Bush's shit and more. Newt spun so much, he could have been one of the four tops from the Motown days. He has the jewelry from Tiffany's, the wives, and the reputation. If Jackoff says Newt is corrupt. Mark it down. Jackoff is the godfather of corruption. When you Google "corruption," Jackoff's picture pops up. He knows all the insiders.

We live in the richest country in the world. Obama's job bill for 447 billion is a modest estimate of what's needed to restore America's reputation as the richest country in the world. The bill should be for two trillion. No one should be unemployed. Economic inequality should not even be an issue in America. Economic inequality is created by legal bribery. When politicians get in bed with Wall Street, their hands are greased.

I have never been to D.C., and don't plan to go, either. I hate pigs. I hate the smell of bacon. I'm sure with all the pigs at the trough on Capitol Hill, the smell of bacon is everywhere. Make room for one more pig at the trough: a hologram from the LDS movement.

The New Civil War

President Barack Obama created a New Civil War by freeing more than five million undocumented immigrants from deportation. Alabama's Rep., Mo Brooks wanted Obama impeached and jailed for five years.

Ted Cruz of Texas is the new General Robert E. Lee. He wants Texas (where there are 2.1 million eligible voters who are not registered) to declare secession from the Union. I guess that's one way of redistricting: remove the whole state from the Union.

President Obama, like Lincoln, just increased his chances of not finishing his second term in office. Ireland's biggest online bookmaker had odds on Obama's first term ending in assassination, with other options available for impeachment and resignation. There are members of Congress today who would lay bets on his assassination, like customers from Ireland and the UK did in his first term.

I'm sure there are some who want to see him do more than five years in jail. They want to see him hung. The odds are we can win this new civil war if the 800 thousand unregistered voters in Atlanta register and vote. We can win this war if the 65% of black voters in Ferguson, Missouri get off their lazy asses and vote. Black people depend too much on others to do for them what they could be doing for themselves.

I remember contacting the NAACP when a white policeman came on to my property in San Diego and threatened to blow my head off for taking out my garbage. The advice I got from the San Diego branch of the NAACP was that I shouldn't live in a predominantly white neighborhood. I see all of these black preachers and politicians going down to Ferguson to show people how to act in civil disobedience to the law. This is not the sixties. That role has already been played, starring Martin Luther King, Jr. Even if this commander-in-chief is assassinated, there will be no shock wave, just a new commander-in-chief, Hillary Clinton, to carry on the battle, with hopefully Elizabeth Warren by her side. The other side of the coin is there won't be a Hillary Clinton if the purple states go back red, because the soldiers are asleep in the battlefields of Georgia, Texas, and North Carolina

Ulysses Grant took back Virginia. Are we willing to give it back in 2016?

Freedom, the American Whore

What does freedom really do for us? Forces us into legal prostitution. Buckwheat once walked into Cheetah's bar and asked a woman who'd just gotten off the pole, "Would you come with me for a million dollars?"

She said, "Yes."
Buckwheat then asked her, "Would you come with me for a dollar?"
She said, "No. What do you think I am?"
Buckwheat said, "Shit. I know what you are. I'm just trying to figure out your value."

America has a price, too. She screws us every minute of the day at the gas pumps, with health care insurances that are junk policies and banks that try to charge you every time you go to an ATM. Shit, I'm always suing Bank of America for something. Some of the whores are Exxon, Mobil, Bank of America, and Union Health Group. Every time politicians take money in some dark room from these companies, they should tattoo that company's logo on their forehead where we would at least know who's screwing us.

Is freedom really free? Hell, no. She's very costly. The biggest cost of all are those young soldiers who think they are fighting wars to protect our freedom. They are fighting and dying for someone else's freedom. The reality is that insurance companies and banks are going to Las Vegas. Las Vegas is in the business of making money and giving back as little as possible. They are fighting and dying for the American Whore machine, the real freedom, big insurance scams, and big banks.

Shit, that's set up like Vegas. You buy insurance, you get sick, and you will most likely get screwed if you are poor and have one of those junk policies. My doctor wanted to do more testing and studies on what she saw as a shadow on my kidney. My insurance was dropped, and they mitigated their losses by refunding me the money I'd paid into the policy instead of the risk of that shadow turning into something that would cost them more. My issue is not unique, just one of the many that someone probably will have litigated all the way to the Supreme Court one day.

Mr. Clarence Thomas sits on that Supreme Court, and his wife is in the Tea Party and advocates for insurance companies. Mr. Thomas should excuse himself from that court. He rode Dr. King's coattail all the way to the highest court in the land, and people wonder why he's a man of few words. Well, he's intellectually dishonest, and if he had any honor and respect for what Dr. King did for him, he would resign from the Court, but he's a coward. He has been on the wrong side of history since arriving at the court. He has a chance to pay tribute to King and allow this sitting president to appoint someone who could be fair and impartial. Black people are the most forgiving people on the entire planet, and if he resigned, black people would give him Harlem.

Judge Thomas is just another power broker. What it really comes down to in the end is that we are all being fucked, and it doesn't matter what party you belong to when they are talking about health care, oil, banking, and housing. Politicians are professional liars, for the most part, and they need power brokers to stay one step ahead of each other in this giant world game of Monopoly.

Obama had to play cards with both parties and deal with power brokers from banks that were too big to fall. We are paying for it with health care, gas, real property losses, and the banks and Mae's are being paid a ransom. I'm sure a lot of us don't understand some of his moves, but he made some good moves with the auto industry and the Bin Laden call. But he still has to deal with some big power brokers who really see us all as only commodities. Obama finally did get the health care bill passed, so if you are poor and just happened to have a shadow on your kidney, you won't become collateral damage in a Ponzi game, of sorts. Bachmann was right when she called the American government *"gangsta."* Bachmann started calling it *gangsta* when the Obamas moved into the White House. Everything about government was criminal well before Obama took office. Power brokers run Wall Street, the banks, and insurance, and it's all criminal. The Jim Crow criminal justice system is locking up the poor for petty drugs and petty crimes, which includes crack cocaine, while white collar crime, which includes powdered cocaine, is given a get out of jail pass in this *"gangsta"* government. Our whole way of life is *gangsta*, and crime has been rampant well before Barack Obama was born.

There is a racially charged disparity between crack and powdered cocaine, as there is between white collar crimes in American institutions that are too big to fall. It's disingenuous to argue over parties and politicians when the laws of this land are corrupted to the core and the political compass usually favors those who buy off politicians, and this goes all the way up to the Supreme Court. America has a whorish slave mentality and couldn't care less about Americans being employed or treated like anything else but whores. Americans don't want to work for minimum wages. America knows that she can outsource to China, India, Vietnam, and almost anywhere in the world and still pay slave wages. Of course, the plan is to break up all the unions. My father didn't belong to a union, and I don't plan to walk in my father's footsteps.

Corporate America buys politicians off on a daily basis. Corporate elites see you as nothing more than someone paying into their treasure chest. They took my policy away from me because my doctor saw a shadow on my kidney, which meant that I might be taking from that treasure chest. I'm willing to bet that no matter how much politicians fight over the debt ceiling, in the end, when the treasure chest is threatened, Wall Street will step in and remind them they are all bought and paid for. That's the whole Congress, Senate, and the POTUS. That's why some of those old white politicians treat Obama like a shoeshine boy: he's bought, just like any other politician. I mean this affectionately with Barrack because I do think his intentions are in a good place, which is hardly ever the case when politics and corporate America meet head-to-head on the same train track.

Chapter Five
The American Dream

I had no one to turn to. I didn't have the Arizona Warrior's family resources to blow the whistle on the Corps. Who would have listened, anyway? The Warrior was rich, white, and a pro football player. I was poor, black, and disorientated with a head injury. I wish I could have taken Joe Monday to Boot Camp with me. He would have opened a can of whup-ass on Sgt. Psycho. Sgt. Psycho was always bragging about his martial arts. Joe Monday would have put little monkey footprints all over his ass.

Once out of that hell hole, I took my grievance to the Department of the Navy, and it fell on deaf ears. Thinking that time brings on change, I tried once more in 2011. I was happy to see the Arizona Warrior's family expose some of the military's behavior. The Department of the Navy's executive director is no better than General Two Star. He was the commanding general at Camp Pendleton. I went all the way up to the base general on a Request Mast. It was like going to see the wizard of Oz.

When I got in front of him, it was like he was not even there, like the wizard hiding behind the curtain. After hearing my complaints, he made the strange fruit joke. The executive director reminds me of the scarecrow. The director also reminds me of the NAACP lawyer I met after filing a harassment case in San Diego: useless. No Marine left behind. I personally know of three who are dead today, dead at the hands of unfit Marines, Marines who were not fit to be in the service. Most of the blacks back on Jackrabbit Hill either ended up in the brig in Fort Leavenworth, dead, or were given a less than honorable discharge. Why? Civil unrest, mostly.

The Corps was back in the sixties with everything, antiquated equipment, racist language that belittled and destroyed morale, poor integration of new recruits, and mixing new recruits out of high school with soldiers right out of Vietnam. Even today, IEDs are sending soldiers home from Iraq dead or with amputated limbs. Jeeps are useless. They're driving around Iraq with IEDs planted everywhere in a jeep that was made for Vietnam. CH-53s and 47s made for Vietnam are useless and too slow.

The Arizona Warrior story. The cover-up. Where is the honor?

The only honor the Corps has is not being caught for the abuse that they call discipline. So they brainwash young recruits with their honor code. The way the Arizona Warrior was treated didn't come as a shock to me. The mistreatment of soldiers is what turned me into a political junkie when it involved civil rights. I can honestly tell you that the Arizona Warrior and thousands of other soldiers died for what they thought was freedom. When your voice doesn't count, how can you be free? There's no freedom left in this country. Everything is bought and paid for, the elections, the Congress, the Senate, and the president. I have posted several warnings on DOD boards about soldiers being put in precarious situations only to have those warning removed. They are dying for a way of life. It's not freedom.

Arizona Warrior's Fire

It came at the break of dawn, piercing the air with no alarm.

A falling soldier in the line of fire. The ultimate sacrifice, the usual lie.

It took a lot of discipline in my struggle to survive while I lay in a pit of blood, fighting for my life. Young men who give their life for this country are meek, the underprivileged who have been sold on fighting for freedom. Sergeant Mad Dog, who most likely received an honorable discharge from the Corps, will go to his grave as an honorable Marine. I will always know the real story.

My father, Rudolph Valentino Hayes, was a meek, selfless, hard-working man. Alcohol was his outlet when he had nowhere else to turn. I only regret that I did not get to know him better. He was a puzzle that I never got to solve. He was around Martin Luther King's age. I wonder all the time if he felt the same way as what MLK preached about: freedom. In my eyes, he slaved his whole life away, then he was gone.

Life goes by so fast. Nothing is free. Freedom is a word for the privileged to use. The unprivileged usually fight. They make the ultimate sacrifices in wars. Freedom is only a dream for many. My father was a poor man; he would give you the shirt off his back. He was also an alcoholic who requested a drink on his dying bed, but he still provided for his family, even from his grave. He was a journeyman in the electric trade, but he was never paid journeyman wages. He never went to college; he had to work. He had to provide for his family. His younger sisters and brothers attended some of the better schools in all of America, the UCLAs and Yales, and received graduate degrees. His sister, Dorothy Hayes, went to Yale University and was mentioned as one of the few black women designers in the USA. Yale University Press, Women Designers 1900-2000.

One of Aunt Dorothy Hayes' first studios in New York

Carmen Hayes did his graduate work at UCLA and returned to Grand Bay before his death. Dorothy and Carmen got the land back in Grand Bay. Dad did not care if his younger sister and brother had it. Dad was selfless. I wish I'd had the courage to tell him not to drink so much and to stop smoking. I felt guilty for not telling him. I would have been disobedient if I had not given him the wine he requested on his deathbed.

My heart aches for my father, who was never given equal pay for his electric skills. I would feel like less than a man not to command equal promotions of the ranks in the Marines. Otherwise, all of my father's sacrifices were for nothing. There's nothing equal about America. The terrorist attack on the twin towers is nothing new to blacks in America. We have a history of it by America on us. It's not just by the KKK, either. It includes all those so-called baseball fans who shouted racist shit at the Colored Comet, the shout that echoed through the State of the Union.

This history is woven into our souls because our fathers, grandfathers, and great-grandfathers made the ultimate sacrifice to America. Our allegiance is not equal because we have never been treated as equals. Ronald Reagan died on the 60th anniversary of D-Day. All I can think of is our defenseless, selfless, poor soldiers storming Normandy shores while Mr. Reagan was probably making out in some Hollywood flick.

Mr. Reagan was our 40th President in the early eighties. After turmoil in the sixties, which bled into the seventies, Mr. Reagan may have contributed to freeing the slaves of communism, but he did nothing to make a difference for apartheid in South Africa or Civil Rights in Mississippi, where the good old boys like Haley Barbour praised the white Citizens Council, aka the White-Collar Klan. The underprivileged usually make the ultimate sacrifice for so-called freedom when they have no idea what freedom really is. It's not being black in America, that's for sure. I know this from seeing the wages my father was paid. My mother would argue with him every week, it seemed, over his paycheck, or lack of a paycheck. The only way I knew how to calm her down was to sing her favorite song, "Ode to Billie Joe." They argued so much, I learned that song by heart. Mike had me singing it to everyone in the neighborhood. I remember,

"It was the third of June, another sleepy, dusty Delta day. I was out choppin' cotton, and my brother was balin' hay. And at dinnertime we stopped and walked back to the house to eat. And momma hollered out the back door 'Y'all remember to wipe your feet.' And then she said, 'I got some news this mornin' from Choctaw Ridge. Today Billy Joe MacAllister jumped off the Tallahatchie Bridge.' "

I believe Mike was a redneck. Those country lyrics calmed her right down. Those were the days: blacks fighting for employment, equal pay. Fighting for rights, fighting for respect. The common black man is still fighting for equality. After surviving the Corps, I waxed my gold Buick Electric Deuce and a quarter and drove into town with some friends, only to be forced out of the car onto the ground at gunpoint on the freeway, then taken to SDPD for prints and mug shots. A sort of "welcome to San Diego" by the Chief of Police. Our only crime was DWB, "driving while black." This was a racist tactic created by the

Chief of Police.

According to the chief, blacks were born to fit a description. The chief admitted years later from his new position as Chief of Police in Seattle that racial profiling was a tactic he'd used in San Diego. In 2011, the hatred spewed up about Barack Obama gave us pause to think back not too long ago when there was a man who spoke just like Barack. It gave us pause to think the unthinkable.

The white noise created by Trump's so-called birther investigation and Wilson's disrespectful shouts at the State of the Union only flame up the Lunatic Fringe, those groups like the KKK. Other losers also attempt the unthinkable. Rep. Gabrielle Giffords is an example of what's coming with all of this hate mongering. Before it's all said and done, Obama will probably be dodging bullets from domestic terrorists (KKK) and Al-Qaeda. When they bring in race as part of their argument, they deserve to be hoodwinked by these professional criminal politicians who are the new General Lees in this class warfare.

Corporate America is all about the color green, and all politicians play their games, both democrats and republicans. The middle class is just trying to hold on to what they have because they got a little sample of what Wall Street could do in 2008, when they crashed this country right into the ground. Whoever it is in the Oval Office, they are bought by high rollers. Obama, too. Goldman Sachs was one of Obama's top contributors, and now he has to explain to the voters why Timothy Geithner is qualified to be Secretary of Treasury when he has spent his life coddling up to the most powerful men on Wall Street. The president also hired Larry Summers. He earned eight million from Wall Street in 2008 when everyone else was losing. I thought the love affair between Obama and Wall Street was finally over until he signed this new debt deal bill on December 16, 2014, which Elizabeth Warren feels benefits Wall Street and not the taxpayers.

The Dark Underbelly of America

America is a slave nation, and electing our first black president has shown a residual amount of racism that's been part of America's history. No president has ever been called a liar in the State of the Union. That's fucking treason to me as a black man. Joe Wilson is not fit for Congress, and his crazy ass Civil War shout in the State of the Union belongs back in a South Carolina graveyard, not in civilized politics. He and those good old southern boys like Mitch McConnell need to be told that the symbol of the south is dead, along with their Battle Flag of the Confederacy.

All of this racist shit that's coming out of the so-called Tea Party is unfortunate. A black man becomes president, and all of a sudden, they lost a country that was never theirs to start with. They want their country back, want another civil war. Robert E. Lee surrendered to Grant. Free speech has shown the world the dark underbelly of America, where the first black president has been called the Anti-Christ, an Indonesian Muslim turned Welfare Thug.

Middle-class and working-class white people started this mob mentality Tea Party because they fear all of the rhetoric that's been going around for years and has resurfaced with the election of Obama. These are the rumors that are created by mostly southern white politicians because their constituents have been feeding off this shit for years. Oklahoma Senator Tom Coburn has joined in with these southern boys, refusing to let the Civil War rest in peace. Mr. Coburn's statement about black men getting handouts is subterranean rhetoric that their constituents down south, from Oklahoma to South Carolina, are wanting to hear because they feel aggrieved and resentful that the federal government is helping bankers, automakers, and irresponsible people who had defaulted on their mortgages.

These are handouts that have nothing to do with blacks. Blacks don't own Bank of America. Blacks don't own General Motors, and very few blacks have mortgages. Corporate America hides behind this type of anti-Obama rhetoric because General Electric, General Motors, and Bank of America have hidden agendas, and none of it works in favor of the middle-class. They are being hoodwinked by politicians who are paid to lie, cheat, and steal by Corporate America. They are politicians who make it their business stealing from the taxpayer.

Joe Wilson has funneled over $181,000 of taxpayer money to his law firm since entering Congress. Mitch McConnell had connections to Jackoff. And then there's Tom Coburn, the right-wing evangelical lawmaker and former roomie of disgraceful former Senator John Ensign at the notorious C-Street residence, who was less than truthful in his testimony to the Senate Ethics Committee. Lying to his constituents is like child's play.

I want to feel sorry for the Tea Party because they are as paranoid as Sir Eric, whom I bump into in a group calling itself the Dilettantes. I had broken away from the so-called De Mau Maus and was dealing black market SIM cards, and Sir Eric was in the black market of voodoo and UFOs, but I usually visit him in his Point Loma apartment for his baked fish and vegetables. I grew tired of all the threats of the De Mau Maus and the parapsychology world of Sir Eric's shit. I just laugh when I think back to the De Mau Maus and Sir Eric.

Politicians will sell their constituents all kinds of bullshit, and most people believe all kinds of bullshit. The Tea Party has been sold a lot of bullshit. People need to understand, it does not matter if you are in the Tea Party, Liberals, or Conservatives: all politicians are whores. Don't let your infatuation with them cloud your judgment.

Obama is claiming to fight for the middle class now. He wants to tax the rich, end corporate welfare, end the wars. It is class warfare, hopefully. Now the middle class has a dog in the fight because the only one I ever knew to fight for the middle-class was Elizabeth Warren. The republicans don't want to tax the rich or end corporate welfare or end the wars, and they are front and centered on their stand.

Now, I can send Joe Monday directly to you and have him slap the hell out of you with that little monkey hand to wake your ass up, or you can just be hoodwinked by this republican dysfunctional family. I know it's hard to give up on the family. Shit, most of those republicans used to be democrats, so they are also like family to me, the creepy side of my family. I mean, everyone has a black racist uncle like Uncle Sherman Cain, who wants to install an electric fence on the border. Now, don't be confused by Sherman's twin brother, Uncle Ben, on the rice box. He's a good guy.

Made In China

We damn sure no longer deserve to be the humanitarian police of the world. We cannot even do the humanitarian thing right here at home. Give the rest of the world a chance to step up. I would suggest Beijing. They are big players in the world market. They should be the humanitarian police for a while. Beijing should take over for us in Afghanistan right now. After all the sacrifices we made for Afghanistan, they reward us by giving oil contracts to China. Why are we still there, borrowing from China to defend them and the rest of the world?

We are the leaders of the free world with antiquated airports, twentieth century train stations, and bridges falling down on top of a Jim Crow Congress that can't get over a black man being the POTUS. Only seven died in the collapsed bridge in Minneapolis; it could have been thousands. There are bridges in worse condition than that of Minneapolis Bridge. There's one in Mitch McConnell's backyard, a crumbling old Ohio River bridge. Senator McConnell made Obama a one-term president even before he stepped into the Oval Office. He would rather see that bridge go down with thousands of his constituents than to past a jobs bill under Obama.

Joe Wilson called him a liar at his first State of the Union. They use all kinds of racist terms referring to Obama: "*Gangsta*" government, the "food stamps" president. They demanded to take their country back. They use all of this racist, coded shit too. As soon as he was elected, I was proud. I also knew that he would gridlock the parties because of Joe Wilson's, Mitch McConnell's, and Tom Coburn's deep-rooted southern hatred. They can't dress it up, code it, or hide it. They open their mouths and their hatred echoes in cyberspace and across the media for all of us to see. We got into this impasse with this do-nothing Congress by going into two wars with no tax increases for those wars. Bush took us into these wars and gave the rich a tax break at the same time.

The only way to break up anti-tax lobbyist G. Dawg's pledge is for the American people to make a pledge of their own: a pledge to vote these self-centered assholes out of office. This is the only way to break up this Washington Monopoly. As a baby boomer, I personally apologize for the generations that came before the boomers, aka OG (Obama generation). It's sad to see a few of them are still around spewing all kinds of hatred instead of paying it forward for the next generation. The Obama generation really wants world peace, and knows the youth of Tehran are no different than the youth in any other major city in America.

Next month, Saj would have lived with me for a whole year, and I find him no different than any other kid in America. He is a healthy, rebellious Iranian kid who likes R&B, hip-hop, and designer clothes, everything a healthy, rebellious American kid likes. I push Saj in school and stay on him as if he were my little brother. He went back to Iran for Christmas. He was anxious to show his moms how to make banana pancakes and a few other meals I shared with him.

If we are going to play hardball with Tehran, we should clean up our own backyard first. Then include Israel, Beijing, and Saint Petersburg. It's a new day and a new time. A warmonger like Senator John McCain wants to build a sub every time Beijing builds a sub. We already have enough shit to blow the world up ten times. When is enough, enough?

The U.S. National Debt runs about $100k every second. If you want to turn back the hands on the debt clock, cut all the fat out of the DOD. Bring the soldiers home from all countries that have been out of harm's way since WWII, like Germany. A strong America is one that's on defense, not offense. Defense is operating at home. Offense is operating from other parts of the globe.

The apocalypse is dead. It dies every time someone pushes their luck a little too far in this free world. People are standing up to bullies all over the Arab spring. In the end, bullies usually get what they deserve. We are still the most powerful country in the world, and we don't have a war hawk in the Oval Office. It's time to take care of America. I'm sure when we are needed, we will be there in a time of need for those who need us. That's just who we are. Those places like Libya, Syria, and Iran are led by bullies. Bullies end up getting what they deserve: death.

Bashar al-Assad is pushing his luck. Places like Beijing and Russia are no longer bullies because it's a new world. Economics is the real war. Beijing has already opened up a can of whoop-ass on us in that area. The cold war is dead. Russians are buying NBA basketball teams. Well, known Russian billionaire Dmitriy Rybolobiev's daughter is only twenty-two, and she purchased an $88 million dollar NYC apartment just to live there part-time. She's also a resident of Monaco and Switzerland.

Kim Jong-Il is dead. The new leader of North Korea is his son, who is a Michael Jordan fan. It's a big new world. The Muslims have their radicals. America has its racist Christian warmongers, also.

Both are a dying breed. The John McCains live to make sure we have soldiers all over the globe. Mitt Romney thinks that Russia is the U.S. No. 1 geopolitical foe. Those days are dead. Somebody needs to tell them that Russia and China are heavily invested in America. The cold wars is dead. Putin maybe felt he was the U.S.'s No. 1 geopolitical foe afterhearing some of Romney's debates with Obama.

Putin made a grave mistake going into the Ukraine. Obama's sanctions against the Russian economy has proved that the No. 1 geopolitical foe idea is not true. Putin's move on the Ukraine only hurts the Russian economy, and that's my reason for saying he's not a geopolitical foe. If Sen. John McCain continues to play these war games, his final resting spot may be a graveyard owned by China. Russia has more money in Europe and American banks than in Russian banks. There's no such thing as a geopolitical foe these days.

Cuba will eventually begin to see the light now that Obama has opened the door for them and closed them to the Russians for being a bully, not a geopolitical foe. The only thing close to a geopolitical foe is China, and that's because Trump is leaving the door open to them doing whatever they want as long as his family benefits.

The Pauls

It's been over forty-five years since Jim Crow laws, and it's hard to believe there are still people on this planet who think like Gov. George Wallace, Bachmann, Gingrich, and the Pauls, just to name a few. People are not hiding behind sheets these days, and the kind of people who vote them into office are people who think like they do.

During the Reconstruction Period of 1865-1877 federal law provided civil rights protection in the South for "freedmen" the blacks who had formerly been slaves. In the 1870s, conservative white democrats gradually returned to power in southern states, sometimes as a result of elections in which paramilitary groups intimidated opponents, attacking blacks or preventing them from voting.

Gubernatorial elections were close and disputed in Louisiana for years, with extreme violence unleashed during the campaigns. In 1877, a national compromise to gain southern support in the presidential election resulted in the last of the federal troops being withdrawn from the South. White democrats had regained political power in every southern state. The conservative, white, Democratic Party redeemer government that followed the troop withdrawal legislated Jim Crow laws segregating black people from the state's white population. The Voting Rights Act of 1965 overruled the remaining Jim Crow laws, and if Rand Paul had his way, private businesses would still be able to discriminate in their restaurants, proving that the apple doesn't fall too far from the tree.

His dad Ron came from that same George Wallace school of thought, with comments like this: "If you have ever been robbed by a black teenaged male, you know how unbelievably fleet-footed they can be." Ron Paul, 1992.

Jimmy "The Greek" Snyder got fired for much less. "Given the inefficiencies of what D.C. laughingly calls the criminal justice system, I think we can safely assume that 95% of the black males in that city are semi-criminal or entirely criminal." Ron Paul, 1992. "We don't think a child of thirteen should be held responsible for a man." Fast forward to 2014. Rand Paul goes to a historically black college and tries to sell a new reason for his remarks on the Civil Rights Act. I witnessed this guy with my own two eyes on the Rachel Maddow show. He clearly felt that private rights are more important than social rights. Rachel Maddow brought up the 1960 Woolworth's sit-in at the lunch counter. He felt that private restaurants had the right to serve who they wanted.

Stranger than Dreams

We are living in very strange times. I had the strangest dream ever. The dream started in the middle of Dr. King's "I have a dream" speech: "...one day, even the State of Mississippi, a desert state, sweltering with the heat of injustice and oppression, will be transformed into an oasis of freedom and justice."

After the word "justice," bells began ringing nonstop at the stock market. Balloons and confetti were everywhere. It was one big party at Cheetah's in Las Vegas with Dr. King, Jesse Jackson, and Richard Pryor. Joe Monday was making it rain nonstop, buying drinks and lap dances for everyone. Girls were on the pole, and girls were all over Richard Pryor. Suddenly I began to choke from laughing so hard at Richard Pryor fighting with Joe Monday over who was going to buy the next round of drinks.

Richard Pryor kept saying, "Nigger, get this little crazy ass albino monkey out of here."

I was choking so hard it felt like I was swallowing my own tongue. I woke up out of desperation for water.

A back page whore had given me a brownie that she got from one of those Medical Marijuana shops that are all over California now. I don't know what kind of weed they put in those brownies. Joe Monday ate most of the brownies, and he was jumping around everywhere. I took only

a couple bites and it had me partying with Dr. King, Richard Pryor, and a two-hundred- year-old monkey, Joe Monday, and waking up with a dry mouth.

Stranger than that was waking up to this crackhead nigger Apostle

85

Claver shouting all kinds of evocative shit about the Democratic Party, getting more than his Andy Warhol's fifteen minutes of fame. Apostle Claver is one of those blacks Ann Coulter was referring to as, "Our blacks are so much better than their blacks."

You can throw in Clarence Thomas, Allen West, and Herman Cain. They have made themselves into cartoon characters who represent that lunatic fringe for White folks. Damn, I guess Ann has papers on these Jim Crow tap-dancing, gospel-singing, tea-serving niggers. That was a wild ass dream. That brownie had some powerful shit in it, or it triggered that Yage shit that's still in my system.

Nothing is strange to me anymore. I grew up in a place where everything seemed imaginary at the Cuba Street property. Everything from pencils falling out of the sky to a monkey named Joe Monday showing up out of nowhere. Not any old monkey, but a levitating monkey who transferred his thoughts to you through telepathic communication. Joe Monday had a sixth sense that detected trouble. He would show up out of nowhere like a genie out of a bottle. I witnessed this for the first time at my girlfriend Tiny French's house. She lived on Adams Street where Chico did a drive-by shooting from a motorcycle, killing Tiny's sister.

Chico pulled up to the house with his AK-47 and sprayed the whole house with bullets. Joe went into action like Mighty Mouse. He threw me off the sofa to the floor before the rounds started hitting the house. He couldn't save Angela. She lay at the bottom of the front doorsteps with a bullet in her head. Joe went on to save me from hurricanes, swamp snakes, gators, and many more times in my childhood, growing up in the campground in Mobile around all those critters and villains.

Chapter Six
Post Jim Crow

Finally, black men are validated for their delusions. This is as close to an apology as we are going to get. It took the death of the Sanford kid, who was just one in a million, to get President Barack Obama to acknowledge the bigotry that has stigmatized young black men in this country since slavery.

Thanks, Mr. President, but we still have a criminal justice system that's not fair to black folks. It was not fair in Florida to the Sanford kid's family. It was not fair in Ferguson, Missouri to the Ferguson kid's family. It was not fair in New York to the man who joked to the dead family.

It's not fair in America. The criminal justice system has too many remnants from Jim Crow laws and needs to be reformed. Congress is so racist that they don't mind that the world sees how they treat this POTUS. They damn sure don't respect him. To them, he's just another Jubilee Nigger who sings Al Green and dances while black folks are being murdered in the streets of America. I wonder from time to time if the president visited Queen and had some of that Yage blown in his face. Maybe he is just having flashbacks to something in his weed-smoking days if he thinks the GOP's Holy Grail is OBAMA CARE. Their Holy Grail is his black ass, and everything he does and says. They treat him like an American negro, Jackie Robinson, or somebody.

His father came to America as a free black man. He's not your typical negro, a descendant of slaves. America has never treated black Americans with respect. It will take Obama two terms as president to understand that his Sidney Poitier's "Guess who's coming to dinner" routine only works for the butler on the big screen. It doesn't work with the Joe Wilsons of Dixie or these redneck lawmakers from Mississippi and Alabama. They wanted to impeach his black ass just for being in the white house. They hate this president with a passion.

Savages from the Cotton Field

The San Diego Police pulled over three of my roommates last week for DWB. Addie told me he did not want to believe he was pulled over for "Driving while Black."

Addie is from Abeokuta. He's young, black, and educated, so why would he believe such a thing still exists? His favorite saying is one this boxing promoter is famous for. "Only in America."

Blacks stem from the cotton fields of that America, which makes us all suspects, which means our credibility will always be doubtful. No one's credibility or character should ever be questioned on demeanor. Demeanor is subjective and biased. We will never be given the benefit of the doubt. Obama is exhibit "A."

I had this blackness debate with my uncle Carmen before he died. I had it with my nephew, and it's one all black people need to have: the debate of how corporate America sees black people. When the cheering stops for that Florida quarterback, they will go after him like a runaway slave. He's lucky the DA's office didn't bring charges.

Ask Iron Tyson how lucky he is. He wore that rag around his head, which I noticed because I used to warn my nephew about the same thing, and he's an engineering student. That rag, do-rags, gold teeth crowns, the braids, earrings, and tattoos are all remnants of slavery, Africa, and Native America. No matter how educated you get, you will still be judged by the book's cover (your culture).

Addie is from Africa and wants to see America through his own eyes. Vicky has my puffy hairstyle from when I was a kid. I notice it's the hairstyle of the son of the newly elected mayor of New York, also. It's the hairstyle of black kids all across America. Vicky is only twelve years old, and her school, Faith Christian Academy, wanted to expel her over this puffy hair look, which we used to call an afro.

When I go to court, I can only remove my earring from my ear. I can't take my crowns from my teeth or change the color of my skin or the way I speak. I'm sure prejudice is the last thing on the minds of Vicky, Addie, and the first black POTUS, but blackness is on trial every day in America. I never, ever believed I would ever see any POTUS as disrespected as I have seen with Barack Obama. The hatred of Barack Obama has set this country back past the Civil Rights Movement.

I used to feel like Addie in the seventies. I went to the best private schools and thought all of that busing black kids to white schools was their problem. I was just a kid. I know now that if it's DWB in San Diego or WWB (waiting while black) at a bus stop in New York or some Tea Party idiot holding a racist sign about Obama, it hurts just as bad as if it were directed at all black people. It's character assassination.

I think we will always be seen as savages in one way or another because of our demeanor, which is being a strong, powerful black man, that people fear. That being said, we will continue to be gunned down in the streets of America. The sad fact is that some of the same areas these black men are being gunned down in—areas like Ferguson, Missouri—are predominantly black with a white DA who's biased towards blacks. The DA of Ferguson recalls his mother being heartbroken after her husband, a policeman, was killed by a black man.

I'm disappointed in black people not doing their civic duty by going to the poles and voting instead of marching in the streets each time a black man lies dead in the street. "VOTE, GOD DAMN IT! VOTE!" Ferguson is 67% black and only 6% went to the polls last election. Ferguson has a police force that's predominantly white and kills young black men like they are savages. They have a system in place that gives the police a license to kill these "savages." They don't have to write up an incident report after killing one of us because they don't see us as humans. Instead, they, "the Ferguson police," get to see everything that's going to be presented to a grand jury then conduct their story around that evidence.

No matter what the facts may say, you have the policeman's word—which is just that, his word—and a DA who will not object to his words, which will be the only words before the grand jury that won't be disputed because hearsay is evidence in this type of hearing. You can almost guarantee that black people on the street who saw what happened would be dismissed as not being reliable due to their own record—authored by the FPD—or they're regarded as just worthless savages who count as nothing but undesirables down there in Ferguson, Missouri.

This history is real, not just in Ferguson, but in Liberia, Nigeria, Saudi Arabia, Iran, and many other countries in the world. The cultural diffusion is like day and night. Black people have been treated like savages since the arrival of the first slave ship to America. I have had guests in my house from Nigeria, Saudi Arabia, and Iran. They have very strong beliefs in their ideas, styles, and religion. I believe their immune systems are even stronger.

I will be the first to tell you that when I have a guest in my house from Saudi Arabia, I can't help but think that all of those terrorists who crashed those planes into those towers were from Saudi Arabia. That's not my biggest problem with them because you have terrorists everywhere. I wish more black people in America were terrorists years ago, like the KKK were.

My problem with the Arabians and the Africans is basic hygiene. Their style builds the development of an immune system where ours suppresses it. I'm not a scientist, but I thought they used the blood of people who were cured of Ebola to combat some of the Americans returning home from West Africa. That's the biggest problem I have inmy house: cultural diffusion.

In 2014, we no longer had a need for the Black Panthers, and if we were going to march, it should've been to the polls. I don't get the right to gun down my neighbor because he feels Obama should be gunned down. Nor do the police get to gun down black men like gorillas in the mist. We must instill a sense of duty in our children. For some reason they don't understand how important it is to have a proper ID and vote. If they continue to act like uncivilized savages, they will continue to be gunned down like that and left in the street to dry up like bush meat. The 2014, midterms were the last straw for me. What good is it to put a black man in the White House then tie his hands behind his back? When you don't do your civic duty and vote, you put your life in the hands of people who don't have a moral compass.

The Court in Black and White

Before the Sanford Neighborhood Watch shooter trial began, I already knew another white man would walk free after killing a black boy. I don't know what's worse: a black boy growing up in the ghettos of Chicago, where black on black crime is a way of life; or growing up in a white neighborhood like Sanford where you are shot down in the streets and the Sanford Police do nothing for days.

I guess you can call me delusional, but black men have always had a problem with homeland terrorists. Most of them carry a badge. Even the most powerful black man in the world, Barack Obama, has a problem with homeland terrorism. He thought just because he got elected to the highest office in the land that America had changed. He found out the hard way in his first State of the Union while the world was watching, when one of those good old boys from South Carolina stood up, that nothing had changed. People in my own block want to see him dead, and I live in California, not Alabama.

I'm well aware of the criminal courts in the military and what they did to young black marines. I'm well aware of the civil courts, both state and federal. I've done my share of pro se litigation and experienced the stigma of being black in those courts. Not much has changed. A black man's life is still taken for granted in the courts. Before they even called one witness in this Neighborhood Watch shooter trial, I felt this jury would be hung, or there would be a jury nullification. It's the south, where bigots are like figs: they grow everywhere down there.

In the criminal justice system, it's a crime to be young and black. I know for a fact if this was a twenty-eight-year-old black man who had shot a seventeen-year-old white boy, he would have been in jail until there was a trial. The Sanford Police would not have let him walk out of their station like they did with the Neighborhood Watchman.

Now that the trial is over, here's my summation: In America, a black football player is given two years in prison for killing a dog. A white man is set free after profiling, chasing down, and killing a black boy. If they bring a Civil Case, G. Ziggy will be forced to take the stand and account for the many lies he has told. My reason for predicting the outcome of this trial prior to its conclusion: bigots.

Juror B-37 spoke with Anderson Cooper in an AC360 Exclusive fifteen minutes after the trial. This juror was speaking to Anderson Cooper about the Sanford shooter as if he was her friend. She spoke of his heart being in the right place. Juror B-37's preconceived ideas and the body language of the Sanford shooter's attorneys prior to the jury coming back with their decision told me all I needed to know. This trial should have never taken place in a venue where everyone in the system is a bigot.

The Sanford Police Department and the DA's office were afraid to mention race. I saw this coming well before a jury was selected down there. It didn't matter that Juror B-37 was condescending when she spoke of the black kid's friend. There were cultural differences when I faced an all-white jury in the Corps. There were cultural differences down there in Sanford. Black people have gotten too relaxed because there's a black president. This case has brought a lot of bigots out to air their thoughts. If anyone understands what I'm talking about, it's the president. These same bigots have been on him since he's been in the White House.

Here's the million-dollar question for Ms. Bigot B-37: when M&M started that four-minute clock, did you ever think once that this kid could have been in a hiding place and too afraid to run home? WHY didn't the law apply to him to stand his ground?

I'm beginning to think that white men think it's their constitutional right to shoot black men down in the streets of America. A right started against rebelling slaves, a right which continued in the cotton fields all over the south. A right that's continued in the streets of America prior to Emmett Till, and will continue way after the Sanford kid. Now we have the weekly shooting of black men. It's ethnocide. If it weren't for DNA, all young black men would be dead or in jail. It would be fucking genocide. But don't pay any attention to me. I'm delusional.

Post Obama's First Term

Déjà vu. I AM, I AM, I AM, I AM, I AM was not only on the signs oppressed black people carried through the streets of Alabama in the Civil Rights Movement. It's been carried in a dark place in my mind from childhood and

was awakened by 9/11. It's carried in my mind every time Smokey sings about it. Every time an act of so-called Islamic Radicalism is mentioned.

Being a black man from the boomer generation, I've had my share of white terror growing up in Alabama and in the Corps. The KKK—homeland terrorists—blew up churches and houses in our neighborhood during the movement, and you couldn't call the police because they were too busy using bull tactics on black folks in the streets of Alabama. They were part of the KKK. The twin towers just brought back personal experiences of terrorism to me. This is NWA, not the Compton group. Just one *Niggaz*. Songonzela is the only reason Oceanside, California wasn't only seconds from burning down one Fourth of July during the riots between black and white Marines. It's been quite a journey. Oceanside is still standing because of the self-radicalization of this one *Niggaz* with the right attitude.

It's too easy to be destructive. There are far too many cowards in the world today. Mad Dog, this Kentucky legislator who turned his back on veterans, and the 112th Congress, they did just as much damage to this country as any terrorist. Mr. Obama finally woke up and started signing Executive Orders to move this country forward. Black people have seen with their own eyes how this first black president has been treated. They call it politics, but black people know what it is. As much as he wants to do things through Congress, it's not going to happen. No matter what Congress is in session, 112th, 113th, they would rather see this country crash and burn than to see a black president get any credit for being one of the most successful presidents ever.

It's happening in real-time. Old bridges are crashing to the ground because our Do-Nothing Congress doesn't like the idea that Obama pointed it out to them. It's gross negligence every time someone has to cross one of these old ass bridges. It's the intentional infliction of emotional distress. It's terrorism. It's a power grab.

We are slowly slipping back into a state of imperialism, colonialism, and racism. This well-known black comedian asked a white boy at one of his comedy shows if he would change places with him. The white boy laughed and said, "No way."

There's always going to be a social stigma for black people, no matter what, and there's always going to be an obsession with this black president. My ninth-grade history teacher made me feel like I didn't belong there when he singled me out for being black and Catholic in a classroom full of white Catholic boys. Electing Barack Obama was supposed to show how far we have come as a nation, but electing him to the highest office in the land is like pulling a scab off an old sore. It just opened up the dark side of humanity.

The Last Confederacy Stand

George Wallace once said, "There's not a dime's worth of difference between republicans and democrats." After this 2012 election, that may have a ring of truth to it. Lincoln recaptured southern properties that declared their secession from the United States. Now that Obama has been re-elected over Mitt "47%" Romney, they want to secede again in 2012. Hillary Clinton will be the new commander-in-chief in 2016, hopefully. I'm sure she will keep this one nation under God. One multicultural nation under God.

From Kentucky to South Carolina, it's a new day. Mitch McConnell,

Joe Wilson and all the other wizards of Dixie should show some civility before going the way of the dinosaur. The whole world had a huge sigh of relief with the re-election of Obama, starting in Latin America, from Caracas to Havana to La Paz. All of Asia and all of Europe joined in the celebration, from London to Germany. The Confederacy had an opposite reaction, starting down on Ole Miss. University campus, where white students protested the election, chanting racial epithets to Hueytown in Alabama where young white folks took to the timelines on Facebook, writing things out of pure ignorance. Mississippi and Alabama are the heart of Dixie. It was expected down there.

No black person will ever forget the first four years of racial hate and profiling of the first black POTUS. Mitt Romney tried to make this election about race headed by John Sununu, Donald Trump, and Reince Priebus, the three stooges. It was ugly before the Civil War, and the nation showed the Confederates and their last standing generals how they felt on November 6, 2012.

The Economy and Small Businesses

The Great Recession officially lasted from December 2007 to June 2008. In 2008 and 2009, the U.S. labor market lost 8.4 million jobs. Unfortunately for my company, Women Designer Clothes, and other small companies like mine, this financial crisis destroyed what it took me years to build. A Do-Nothing Congress only made things worse by playing a game of fucking chicken with the debt ceiling. No other sitting president has ever been threatened this way with the debt ceiling. The hatred of this president is incredible. If a white president received the Nobel Peace Prize, saved the Car Industry, and caught and killed Osama, they would be calling him King Midas.

Everyone around the world knows that the ongoing battle in Washington with this first black POTUS is partially precipitated by race, and I would personally add envy. They envy the mere idea of his success. We have been trying to get our health care system reformed since FDR, some eighty years. Obama did it, so now they—let's call them the new minority fringe, for now—feel it will destroy America, which is just the opposite of how the CBO feels.

Seems like we have been here before with Social Security and Medicare. I once said they would rather see this country burned to the ground than work with Obama. It's too bad. We could be in a very healthy economy. Instead, we have this political gridlock shit that has destroyed the economy. Obama has been in office six years now, and republicans will use the Ayn Rand playbook on him until he's out. One way to put it is, Ayn Rand teaches you how to use cognitive bullshit dissonance, or in simpler terms, be a pathological liar. The Do-Nothing Congress has mastered doing just that, nothing, and blames Obama for the sky falling. They don't want a jobs bill, a health care plan, or anything under this president, and we end up with a poor economy and small Mom and Pop businesses like mine suffering from this political bullshit.

I started my company from the ground up, and I can tell you firsthand that "frivolous litigation" is a myth created by corporate America to deny you the right to a fair trial under the 7th Amendment. Tort Reform only protects corporate America. Obama bailed out the banks, and I understood in return that the banks were supposed bail out small businesses and get America back to work. Bank of America took some of that bailout money, which was taxpayer's money. They were supposed to work through the SBA ARC loans program, which the government-backed 100%. I applied for an ARC loan through Bank of America and found out that they did not support the program. It was just another con job.

My mother floated me a small personal loan, which is protected by her mortgage through B of A, instead of the money that should have been available through Arc. The antipathy created by public pronouncements, those lauding support for small businesses, is the key to job creation. I started from a small boutique dba Mischievous Cliche out of college, and took that company to the internet as Women Designer Clothes, where I was able to reach a lot more customers without the traditional overheads.

Small businesses that had no government connections or political connections had no chance of getting an SBA loan. During that same period of time, when I was trying to get an Arc loan, Michele Bachmann and her husband received $30,000 from Minnesota and the federal government for a business that had questionable counseling. Marcus Bachmann came out of the closet long enough to call gays "barbarians." This is Exhibit A, which is why I call all politicians liars. The Bachmanns call themselves a Christian counseling practice, and the world saw exactly what I saw: a gay man calling another gay man a barbarian. Is he fit to give the clinic's employees mental health training? Which is what Michele said the money was used for.

This is just as bad as William Jefferson hiding $90,000 in his freezer. This has no use for the SBA because banks couldn't care less about you keeping your house if it's in foreclosure, or your business, unless your name is Bachmann or Kushner, someone who may have some say on putting more of your tax dollars into these institutions that are too big to fall. Michele is right when she calls the government "*gangsta.*" However, her timing is off by acknowledging it under the Obama administration. Where is Michele now when the real *gangsta* government is in control and Trump and his son-in-law, Jared Kushner, are doing all types of loans right in the White House? Trump will never go after China for intellectual property law violations if they open their purse to his son-in-law, who invested in the Devil's House at 666 5th Avenue.

However, my small business can be tied up in Trademark litigation based on something China made with the blessing of some of these

American companies. Lending has more to do with who you know and who you are. Fraud is built into all parts of government, from customs all the way up to corporate welfare. This is the kind of corruption that America doesn't want to believe, but you only have to open your eyes. Look at the evidence: Exhibit A, Bachmann & Associates. Here you're overspending that the Tea Party is crying about by one of their leaders. Exhibit B, William Jefferson, your typical fraud case.

I can go on and on because this type of *gangsta* government has been around well before Obama was born. Michele Bachmann suddenly fits this administration with her *gangsta* government title, along with the rest of her slavery comments. Her comments are racist, she's not fit for office in this day and time. She is holding on to the vestige of slavery because that's all she and her Tea Party has left in a society that has passed them by. Their racist feelings are depicted all over their monkey signs, and her personal feelings about this president are just as juvenile. She's not alone.

Newt's reference about the first food stamps president is racist. These racists have all but destroyed this economy because their main focus is to get their country back, meaning their priority is to remove this black president from the White House. Michele Bachmann is a Tea Party patriot. Her main fights are supposed to be for "overspending," and she's been putting government money into her and her husband's business since 2006, that we know of. I also wonder if she received a student loan herself. Her claim is that the money went to train people in her company. How do you complain on one hand about student loans being "overspending," and then claim that the government loans that your company got went to training people in your company? I guess all student loans are overspending, unless they benefit Bachmann and Associates. Seems like a conflict of interest for her Tea Party.

A real business like mine has no use for the SBA or the government. It's just a hanging shingle to us, because that institution has no control of the banks that are supposed to be working with small businesses on Arc loans such as mine. Customs charged me a 25% tax on goods coming in and 2% on goods going the other way. I'm too small to be of any concern. So, I'm overtaxed by customs to bail out B of A, who won't give me an Arc loan, but if somehow money was made available to Bachmann & Associates under the SBIR, then I'm also paying for her to convert gays under her Christian counseling so-called business.

I knew back in the eighth grade, when I was fishing for blue crabs and lady legs, that people had to work and spend to create a healthy economy. I did my part by supporting the Jewish market back then. Times have changed. People are selfish and don't care whether someone can have the same opportunities that existed because of the Pell Grants and loans that helped educate people so they could have opportunities to work and consume. My business is in the red because consumers are not making as much as they were making before the Bush wars, which means consumers are not buying and the market is unhealthy. Instead of corporate America going after China, they come after the small businessmen for Trademark copyrights instead of going after China for intellectual property violations. What happens in the end is companies like Apple and True Religion are forced to do business with China, and neither DJT nor any POTUS can do anything about it because America owes China billions.

An SBA loan is made believe for someone like myself. I'm not General Motors, so I'm not going to get bailed out, but I wonder if some of those republican fat cats sitting on the GM Board changed their stripes when Obama bailed them out, or did they just go on taking corporate welfare while riding around with their noses turned up at poor people getting the same handouts?

Our problem is republicans like Senator Mitch McConnell, whose main objective was to get Obama out of office instead of creating a job bills to put people back to work. Mitch McConnell was included in Crew's 2007, 2008, and 2009 reports on congressional corruption for exchanging earmarks for campaign contributions by clients of his former Chief of Staff. He's no better than one of those GM republican fat cats with their hands out. However, he has his nose turned up at Obama.

His Tea Party friend, Michele Bachmann, is fond of calling Obama a socialist and echoing Mitch McConnell's theme of making him a one-term president. Truthdig called her a "Welfare Queen" for receiving over

$251,000 in federal subsidies on her farm, $137,000 Medicaid funds for Bachmann and Associates, and over $417,000 from Freddie Mac in 2008 on her house, just weeks before denouncing them. Obama has been one of Michele's targets, with all kinds of racist rants. She accused Huma Abedin, a thirty-seven-year-old Muslim American born and educated right here in the USA, of having connections to the Muslim Brotherhood of Egypt. Michele is a paranoid racist who's not fit for Congress.

America is becoming more diverse each year, and there's just no place for xenophobic clowns like Michele Bachmann. She's a clown, her stage is Congress, and she should be the Joker in the Batman movie. I mean, when you elect people who are living on the same welfare that the Tea Party denounces, then you should understand why the Tea Party is so naive. The McConnells and Bachmanns are small fish that have set this country back. The Big Fish is Mitt Romney, who has been outsourcing American jobs to China since 1998. Now he's running for president and wants to tell you that he knows how to create jobs for Americans. Mr. Romney hasn't done anything wrong. He just doesn't care if Americans or Chinese are working the lines. His bottom line is what he puts in his Swiss bank account. He's not doing anything different than Apple, Ralph Lauren, Nike Inc., GE, and many others. However, those companies are not running for the office of president and lying about their outsourcing.

The Tea Party is not the only ones that's naive. I can't win for losing. I found myself on Jackrabbit Hill when the Vietnam War was basically over, but it was just beginning for me. Second Battalion, 5th Marines, 1st Marines Division was returning home from Vietnam, and they brought that war all the way home to Jackrabbit Hill. I never knew how racist people were until I was integrated into this unit coming from Vietnam. This was raw racism, not my ninth-grade history teacher reminding me that I'm black, not Brother Foster degrading me because I was black, not Sgt. Gugle degrading and assaulting me because I was black. This was raw and something I did not see or just didn't want to see in Alabama.

The Catholic nuns protected me from Alabama's culture most of my young life. I only heard stories about Vietnam and was glad I wasn't there. I guess it did not matter because Vietnam had brought the war to me when a Vietnamese blew up a building in San Diego where I had my first business, a boutique called Mischievous Cliche. Now I know what those preachers felt like when they were firebombed.

This Vietnamese man was a product of that war, but he was only one man. I guess he could have changed me as a person, but then I would be just another hater like my ninth-grade history teacher, Rep. Steve Scalise, Sgt. Gugle, and all those lost Marines on Jackrabbit Hill who killed my best friend with that shit they were selling like they were in the middle of some fucked-up city. We were on a Marine Corps base.

No matter what I've experienced in Alabama—the Corps and my own store being blown up—nothing hurts worse than to continue to sabotage an already sick economy by not working with the president. None of it has been able to make me feel any different from when I was swinging from tree to tree in my backyard with Joe Monday protecting me from all the little trolls. My business was doing just fine until the

Great Recession of 2008, without Trademarks from China like Ivanka. Trump vowed to save ZTE soon after she got those Trademarks. B of A would not give me an SBA, but they did give some to U.S. Rep. Michele Bachmann, and I'm willing to bet my portfolio was a lot better than hers. Small black businesses like mine don't get handouts, but you can bet that white women like Ivanka and Michele did.

Goodbye Joe

Not until Thursday, May 23, 2013, did "Nanny" Leona Johnson's spirit finally leave the Cuba Street property with Granny, her daughter. My nephew heard me hollering in my sleep for Mike. He knocked on my door and asked me if everything was okay. His knock brought me back from the Cuba Street property, where I was standing in the dining room when something real cold went through my body and out the window. I think it was Joe Monday's way of saying goodbye. I think Nanny was Joe Monday. She finally convinced Granny to leave the Cuba Street property. She came back as Joe Monday, I believe. She came back as Joe Monday so I wouldn't be too afraid of her. She knew the last time we were together, she levitated me right off her front porch.

I was the only one with her daughter, Granny, when she died. Her way of thanking me was through Joe Monday. Granny's spirit was trapped in the bedroom across from the dining room, which had no escape routes when she died. The windows were closed, the fireplace was burning. I'm guessing Joe Monday must have thought it was important for me to know that Granny had finally left that old house. It was her house, and it was no longer the house it was when she was alive. Ghosts know when it's time to go.

Nanny had nothing left in Mobile. Her Pecan Street property had been gone for years. Nanny had nothing here and everything on the other side, and finally convinced Granny to go with her to the other side. I wanted to call Ricky because he was the only sibling left in the Cuba Street property when she finally left. I didn't want to alarm him.

Her house was far from the beautiful home we'd grown up in as kids. When I went back in my dreams, I didn't know if I screamed because of the spirits going through my body or just seeing the neighborhood die. Nothing was the same in that neighborhood. Everything was dead or dying. The big pecan tree in the backyard where I had my tree house and hung my first Tarzan rope was gone. The magic peach tree, gone. My award-winning collard greens garden, gone. Hurricane Betsy destroyed the huts that were at the end of our backyard on the Cuba Street property on her way through Mobile. Now everything else is gone, also. It would take the supernatural power of the Queen of Voodoo herself, Marie Laveau, and all the slave spirits from the Clotilde to remove the curse that's killing a place that was once magic to me.

Rigged

I was building ships at the age of fifteen. Boys today are still playing video games well into their thirties, and this is the new universe. Boys hold on too long to video games and comic books.

The Corps wasn't ready for me. The Corps' so-called discipline had no structure and was locked in some kind of slavery time zone where the base general found it okay to make jokes about hangings. Civil disobedience was my way of saying, "Don't treat me like I'm three-fifths of a freaking dog."

I never needed to be motivated by anything in my life. If you treat men like animals, they will act like animals. None of these new recruits needed this old Marine Corps' gung-ho discipline in platoon 2115. They also did not deserve to be around Marines with PTSD who had mental breakdowns like Private Psycho and Sgt. Gugle.

I was blindsided by the attack on me by Mad Dog while doing bends and thrust into a pit at MCRD. Mad Dog came up behind me and hit me in the head with the butt of my M-14. It was an extraordinary event which took more than my natural powers to survive. I don't know how I'm still here today. Maybe I'm just a strong slave who can't be killed, or Joe Monday or someone was looking out for me.

I just know I took that anger with me to Jackrabbit Hill, where it was met by a lot of blacks with anger. I'm still mad after all this time, and somewhat delusional. I sacrificed a lot in my life to get out of high school, which meant working after school on the campus and building ships in shipyards in the summertime as a kid. It was a cowardly act, a hate crime for me to be called a nigger and attacked by a drill instructor. I was seventeen and joined the Corps to get away from shit like this in Alabama.

MCRD is the angriest I've ever been in my life. I got nowhere with my grievance in the Corps, so I wrote the Board for Corrections of Naval Records. I was informed by the Board for Correction of Naval Records that, "Although at least some of the evidence you have submitted is new, it is not material." My guess is that the Board is worried about Sgt. Gugle honor. What about my honor, Mr. Executive Director? What about your honor? Does anyone ever do the honorable thing anymore?

Well, it's a new day and the millennial generation may bring new hope. Which means a lot to me, coming from a generation that saw everything in black and white and colored. I was a real all-American boy. Played football up to the eighth grade, which is when I began to take on jobs to pay my own way through life. Which meant football had to take a back seat to building ships on Pinto Island and picking up trash around campus to pay for tuition.

I joined the Corps, suffered a head injury in boot camp, but started back playing football for the Corps in between fighting for basic human rights and rights for my fellow Marines at a time when they weren't being fairly promoted through the ranks and racial issues were at an apex in the Corps. I guess the Corps was trying to shake the sixties. Now I feel like I have shackles on my ankles, a gift from the Corps.

I was just out of high school and had worked very hard to succeed to this point in life. The Corps was just another stepping stone. None of us in Platoon 2115 deserved the treatment of Sgt. Gugle, nor being put on an unfit base right out of boot camp. Out of the frying pan and into the fire: Jackrabbit Hill.

In the south as a kid, racism didn't hit me too hard because I was too young to understand all that bigotry coming from the mouths of the Bear and Governor Wallace. They were just characters to me, like some of the floats in the Mardi Gras parade. I guess having the San Diego Police Department draw their guns on me twice was alarming, when I think about it, especially when I see black kids gunned down these days on a regular basis. Because now I know it was directly related to profiling. I also know that the San Diego NAACP was no better than those officers who drew their guns on me.

In my case against the United States Marines Corps, I did nothing for years because I knew what the outcome would be. All of our laws are rigged because you have Jim Crow remnants left in a system that was meant to treat a certain part of our society unfairly. Those unfair advantages do not begin to describe how biased the Prosecuting Attorney Jim Crowed that grand jury in Ferguson, Missouri. The sad thing about that whole state of affairs is that black folks destroyed their own community. I destroyed the Marine Corps community. They got to wake up to the destruction they did. White folks don't have to wake up to that destruction in their neighborhood. It gives the trolls over at so-called news channels like Fox and that "Morning Clown" on MSNBC ammunition to keep talking about shit that's unfair to start with. How can you even begin a debate on race when even the instructions that were given to the grand jury in Ferguson were wrong?

White folks who talk out of both sides of their mouths are trolls. They love to talk about how savage we are. The Ferguson DA got one thing right in his speech to the Nation: it's a tragic story. A tragic story he created protecting a rogue cop and demonizing a black boy who was nothing more than a juvenile delinquent, which most teens are. It speaks volumes about our legal justice system now and back when I was in the Corps.

After the riots subside, there should be significant consequences with the Ferguson Police department, starting with the resignation of the chief of police for allowing his officers to use bull tactics. Then increase the hiring of minority officers. Do an analysis of excessive force. There should be a loss of support of an absentee mayor and the governor for not removing the DA once he told the story about a black man killing his mother's husband, who was also a Ferguson police officer. There should be an analysis of the general political and economic atmosphere that continues to contribute to black men being ambushed in the streets of America by rogue cops.

Two New York cops were ambushed like the kid in Cleveland was when two cops rode up on his shooting. Ambushed like the young man holding a toy rifle in a Walmart store. Ambushed like the man choked to death on the streets of New York by a gang of thuggish cops. I can go on and on how black men have been ambushed on the streets of America by the KKK and rogue cops, all the way back to Emmett. My court-martial was a kangaroo court. This grand jury in Ferguson was a kangaroo hearing. What makes these types of hearings kangaroo hearings are the Jim Crow tactics that allowed a Ferguson DA to wrongly interpret a 1985 Supreme Court decision in the case of Tennessee vs Garner, and the handling of evidence by the shooter himself.

Trolls that speak out of both sides of their mouths over at the Fox Rumor Mill, they don't care about the facts in most of these shootings. They just side with the police, which has already dirtied the waters with Jim Crow tactics (see DOJ findings for Ferguson police department). The findings basically show that poor black folks pay to run major cities off of these types of DWB stops. Corporate America is racist.

A media conglomerate hired an all-white cast for his movie, a religious story. He said, "Every Egyptian he ever knew looked white." I wonder if he had ever met Muammar Gaddafi. He damn sure doesn't look white. Gaddafi looked like some of my Cajun cousins.

The bottom line is most of the people who run corporations are people like this media conglomerate. He bankrolled his movie, and if he wanted an all-white cast, it's his production. Discrimination is the foundation that America was built on. It's institutional racism. It's alive in America, promoting whites to top positions in major football universities year after year and hiring a token black coach every blue moon to look like some kind of progress is being made with black folks. It's a gerrymandering game.

The same media conglomerate who brought you a religious story with an all-white cast—because he never saw an Egyptian who wasn't white—brings you Fox News, which broadcasts only conservative political positions and has had a biased position on the side of white officers in every white officer shooting of blacks, and a white neighborhood watch volunteer who killed a black kid and got away with murder. I'm sure everyone in America knows about the real former neighborhood watch volunteer by now. He got away with murder and continues to find trouble in Sanford with the police being called. The criminal justice system has always been rigged with remnants from the Jim Crow era.

Self Defense

According to archives at Tuskegee Institute, the last documented hanging of a black man down south was in the late sixties. That Tuskegee study needs to be revised. Do bears shit in the woods? Did slaves eat chitterlings? Was Little Red Riding Hood really a whore? Did they still hang black men in the woods after 1968? The answer is yes to all of the above. Not only do they still hang them in the woods, but the police also shoot them down like prey in the streets of America.

Joe Monday told me he personally knew Little Red. He noted, "She was a shiftless, lazy, white French whore who ran through the woods in a red mini skirt and heels, fucking with the wolves." Little Red was a beautiful little nymph whom all the wolves drool over eating. Tricks all over the woods wanted Little Red. She was the hottest doll in the woods. She had a Django pimp that was eaten by the wolves. Then she was at the wolves' beck and call.

I asked Joe Monday, "How in the fuck do you know Little Red Riding Hood?"
He said, "I met her great-granddaughter on a pole in Cheetah's."

Now, why would a white French whore be running through the woods in 1927? Joe Monday had some strange tales. Seven years later, in 1935, after Little Red stopped running in the woods, Mike was born in the Dirty South, Mobile, Alabama. Unemployment was around 20.1%, which meant more than just niggers were eating chitterlings. Persia was renamed Iran and the Babe hit his 714th home run. Jackie Robinson was only sixteen years old and could only dream of being in the Major League one day.

Now, let's fast forward to Mobile, Alabama in 1981, when a young black man was abducted in downtown Mobile and hung by the KKK. Here recently, in 2015 in Port Gibson, Mississippi, another black man was found hanging. Before that, it was North Carolina in 2014. I was a very young man in my teens and knew not to go through Mississippi unarmed. If black men are going to continue to live in the woods of thesouth, they better defend themselves, legally or illegally.

There is precedence for self-defense. In 1985, Sagon Penn was pulled over for DWB in San Diego, like I and so many other black men had experienced through the seventies. I patronize Sagon Penn's grandfather's restaurant in San Diego on many occasions. Sagon worked there, and this kid was a model for what young black men should be like.

His grandfather was Muslim and raised Sagon to be respectful of everyone, including the police. This kid was the softest-spoken kid I had ever met when he waited for me at his grandfather's restaurant. The SDPD had quite a history of DWB stops that Chief Kolender justified by saying, "Blacks was born to be suspects."

From 1975 until that night in 1985, ten constant years of harassing young black men in San Diego. Young Sagon was pulled over and dragged from his car by the police, where a fight began. The police officer went for his gun, which Sagon ended up with and shot the officer in self-defense. A San Diego jury later found him not guilty.

The police departments were full of the KKK back in Alabama in the sixties, and I'm sure they are full of racist assholes today. If there's a KKK member sitting in Congress, why would I be surprised by racist text messages by police in the Fort Lauderdale police department? Now that the DOJ has dug up evidence of how cities like Ferguson have been funded by poor black people over the years, there seems to be something to that John Conyers HR 40 bill for reparation.

Chapter Seven, Part I
The Color of Authority

Nigger" is a word that is mostly used to degrade black people. My take on the word is that it has nothing to do with the color of your skin. I don't believe that black folks are African Americans. We are just Americans. Haven't we sacrificed enough for this country in slavery, hangings in trees, and jail cells all over the south? Niggers are at the bottom of that Tallahatchie River in Mississippi and there have been savage slaughters in black churches, starting with those three little girls in Alabama, now South Carolina. This shit is all over Dixie wherever that Confederacy flag exists. It's a license to kill niggers.

Texas police killed my baby brother, as far as I'm concerned. He was born on Christmas Day. I took his ashes and wrapped them into a rainbow assortment of gifts and took them to Mary, Star of the Sea, and asked for her blessing before burying him in the Pacific. I'm glad my dad is not around to see this shit.

Rudy, my dad, was a black man. His dad, Earl, was a black man. Earl's dad, my great granddad, was a black man. None of these black men in my family can be traced to the Clotilde or any slave ship. My granny, Mary "Mamma" Scott, had as much Creek blood in her as any other Native American. The Creek tribe resided in Georgia,

Alabama, Florida, and North Carolina until they were forced to move to Oklahoma in the 1800s. Mamma's roots are traced back to Creek Natives and New Orleans French Cajuns.

Niggers were here before the Clotilde docked. Columbus was a nigger. Niggers are not black folks, just fucked up folks like Columbus, Supreme Court Justice Clarence Thomas, and Donald Trump. Rachel Dolezal is white, but I see her as black because she sincerely sees herself as black. Anyone who's white and wants to walk in a black person's shoes deserves to be black. Black folks are mixed with so much shit that really no one knows what the fuck we are these days. White men raped slaves and Natives just for the fuck of it.

I know one thing for sure: I'm not African American. Does Mary "Mamma" Scott look like she's from Africa? She married a very lucky man, Willie Scott. He was my granddad, and the reason I legally changed my name to Chase. He also told me about a plot to poison General Robert E. Lee through his cook, who was a slave. His granddad told him about the plot, and he passed it on to me.

Then there was the story about three boys who were hung on the Cuba Street property. These boys became fixtures on the property, ghosts. They played their ghost tricks on me several times while growing up as a kid on that property. They made pencils fall from the sky. Shot marbles with me and Joe when they were not invited. They were really friendly, mischievous ghosts who were hung because they tried to run away from their slave owners and were caught on the Cuba Street property. They help with my garden which grew collards, corn, and peas. They had fun playing ghost games as a joke on me.

Joe Monday got a kick out of actually seeing them pull these tricks on me. I knew they were around, but I could not see them. Joe was a ghost too, but I could see her. I saw her because she wanted me to see her. I believe a ghost has that choice, if it wants to be seen or not. I remember Nanny's eyes as a kid, and Joe had Nanny's eyes. Joe was a reincarnation of Nanny, an old French Creole Indian, my great-grandmom who came back as this little white monkey, Joe Monday.

I haven't made it through one life, and I have been a nigger, a negro, colored, black, and now African American. I prefer to be just a fucking black man. Look at these ISIS niggers. Those jihad lone wolf motherfuckers got those war hawking trolls all fucked up. The birth of that shit was during the shock and awe attack on Iraq. ISIS is the remnants left over from that war in more ways than one. America went over there and tried to shape Iraq in the image of America. No matter how many troops we send over there to train those people, they will always drop their guns and run. They don't want to be shaped in the image of America. They have their own history.

People all over the world know that niggers have been running from authority since the Clotilde docked off the Mobile Bay. American footprints are now all over Iraq when there never was probable cause to be there to begin with.

When I grew up in Mobile, we had more professional black people there at that time than today. Some parts of Mobile have regressed to just another war zone like Iraq. A lot of ghettos in America are war zones: Mobile, Ferguson, Cleveland, Baltimore, and New York, to mention a few. Every year, young black people are born into these destitute war zones in America, where white cops are the enemy due to DWB stops, shakedowns, and unconstitutional harassment. These are basically young black people who are collateral damage due to the war zone they were born in.

We can't get it right in America, even after a Civil War, so how in the fuck can we go to another country and try something we have been failing at for years in America?

Niggers are not protected by the constitution in New York. They are searched under the color of authority for being anything but white. Donald Trump has been profiling Obama since he's been in the White House. All that racist shit Donald Trump talks about, repatriation with the Mexicans, and the border is nothing new. Almost everyone in the Republican Party is known for this racist shit. Electing the first black president should have been something very positive going forward for race relations, but what's left in my mind is Obama being called the food stamps president, a tar baby, an Indonesian Muslim turned welfare thug, and that his parents were monkeys, and all of this shit was said by people in Congress or some other parts of our government. And we wonder why Vladimir Putin doesn't respect Obama.

No commander-in-chief has ever been disrespected like Obama. Mike Huckabee compared Obama to Adolf Hitler with his statement of the Iran nuclear agreement. This so-called preacher and ex-governor of Arkansas states the agreement was marching the Israelis to the door of the oven, a comparison to the Nazi concentration camps. The southern states eat up that shit. Trump and the Republican Party have been serving them since Obama has been president.

I try not to put too much on the color of a person's skin because I know niggers come in all colors. For example, I prefer to have a white woman, Rachel Dolezal, represent me in a Civil Rights proceeding than a black man who has no passion about being black, which I've seen a lot in the NAACP over the years.

I have no fucking idea why anyone would think Supreme Court Justice Clarence Thomas is black. You have house niggers all over America. We have them in Congress, the Senate, on the Supreme Court, and in every police department in America. Niggers haven't stopped running since they jumped off the Clotilde in Mobile Bay, and at the way they are being shot down in the streets of America like animals in Africa, I can only say, "Run, nigger, run."

Black people seem to be shocked every time a hate crime is committed down south. Niggers don't have too many choices in the ghettos of America. Selling drugs is one of those choices, the most evil choice of them all, because they are selling that shit to mostly black people. Black people are collateral damage caught up in these war zones, fighting the evil of drug-pushing niggers and racism by white cops.

115

As long as that Confederacy flag is allowed to fly over the state of South Carolina, they should not be shocked by anything. That Confederacy flag is a symbol for the Civil War, a symbol for the Clotilde and slave owners, which was also our founding fathers all over this fucked up land. A symbol for Ferguson, Cleveland, and for hate crimes all over America.

Robert E. Lee had a change of heart after the Civil War and wanted that Confederacy flag put down. I guess that's how his name, "Robert Lee," got into our family, but it had to stop with me. Mom should have just named me George Wallace. He supposedly had a change of heart, too.

Domestic terrorism is part of America like hot dogs, baseball, and apple pie. The Confederacy flag and the ISIS flags are no different. They are both symbols of terror. We spent millions of dollars going after terrorists who killed under the black ISIS flag, and not one red penny going after the terrorists who killed black people under the Confederacy flag.

If bodycams had been on the police all over the south since the 1960s and in their small jail cells, you would understand what I mean by black people killed under that Confederacy flag. My dad, Rudy, and MLK missed out on a lot: the first black president, and hopefully the beginning to the end of that fucked up Confederacy flag in South Carolina and anywhere else they fly that flag or wave it down south.

I hate to admit this, but my first hero was MLK, and Donald Trump was second around the time he wrote, The Art of the Deal. Now he's public enemy number one. He, the Donald, is the biggest con artist in the world, which is what made him my hero. I saw him as a twentieth-century Robin Hood type, who hustled the establishment at their own games. People down south are so fucking gullible to believe the scams

Donald Trump is pulling. He, the Tea Party, and Republican Party deserve each other, because to hear this man shouting from Mobile to Dallas reminds me of the grand wizard of Oz shouting loud and saying nothing is behind that curtain. If I close my eyes and listen to Donald Trump, it's George Wallace from behind the Magnolia Curtain of Dixie, or Joseph Stalin when he continued to go after Hillary.

Chapter Eight
Final Thoughts

We had more black folks in prison in 2015 than we had slaves in 1850 in America. Black Lives Matter (BLM) met with Hillary Clinton on her campaign route in 2015. Hillary asked BLM what is it that they wanted. Let me suggest to Hillary some of my final thoughts. First, pardon all the black lives for the bill her husband signed that put blacks in prison on racist cocaine laws: powder vs rock. Second, reparations. Not for the Atlantic slave trade, but for institutional discrimination that punishes blacks unfairly, as shown by the Justice Department's findings in Ferguson. How many Fergusons are there in America? (It's not really reparations; it's money that was taken from black folks and should be given back with interest). Third, before thinking about how to bring in more homeless immigrants, let's make sure there are no homeless veterans in America, regardless of their discharges. Not all discharges are equal due to the same discrimination found in the military's ranks, as I pointed out in a previous chapter. Fourth, Citizens United, which I like to refer as Citizens Divided, has done so much harm to politics and government. The only hope for this country is for Hillary Clinton to become president and appoint a couple more Supreme Court Judges to the Court and find a way to overturn Citizens United vs. FEC.

I've never seen another President go through the shit I have seen Barack Obama go through. During his first State of the Union, Joe Wilson started another Civil War when he called the commander-in-chief a liar. Joe Wilson started a tide of rebellious attacks on this commander-in-chief, with his foot soldiers marching and the Tea Party closing ranks around him demanding their country back. America is on a stage for the whole world, and Putin has been watching with a tub of buttered popcorn and a Diet Coke. As a matter of fact, Putin had a front row seat. Putin is smart enough to understand how big the partisan divide could be. He also understood how part of America would never accept a black man as the commander-in-chief, which is why he is in Syria and the Ukraine. I still see Putin as just another gay boy in the Russian navy. I definitely don't see Russia as America's biggest geopolitical foe.

Over the years, the USSR has had some of the greatest chess players. Vladimir is not one of them. His bellicose moves in today's world will cause the collapse of Russia quicker than the collapse of the Soviet Union. Vladimir would have shown a lot more respect to this POTUS if he hadn't seen Joe Wilson and all the Tea Party in Congress disrespect him on a daily basis. A birther clown like Donald Trump can profile the most powerful man in the world because he's black. Donald is not a patriot. He and his Tea Party (backed by Congress) has weakened the office of the POTUS to the point that America is not taken seriously anymore because of the reality clown show that's seen around the world on a daily basis. It saddens me to think that a lot of these clowns are home-grown down in Mobile, Alabama.

I learned as a kid that anything can grow in that black soil in Alabama: cotton, watermelons, and clowns like Congressman Mo Brooks and Congresswoman Martha Roby. Finally, I don't know if Hillary will listen to me, the BLM, or anybody, but I do know that niggers like Columbus, Trump, and Colonel Allen West hate women.

They think it's funny to demean them by joking about their periods and attaching their names to stories that make women nothing more than an oral relief station for men. Columbus raped and demeaned women of color for fun. My hope is that women will do a lot of research before the 2016 election, because running onto a stage to be groped by someone like Donald Trump, who sees them as a stupid oral relief station, is really funny. Fox News should not have asked Donald Trump for an apology for joking about Megyn Kelly's period. Their station has never once asked Donald or any of their guests to apologize for something that their network does all the time: demean people.

For example: on Columbus Day in 2015, Fox News Red Eye joked about white men with guns raping women of color in 1492. Fox News gave birth to Donald Trump's politics and raised him on their network. Everything he knows about politics comes from that evolution over at that network. Evolution is a fact. For most republicans, facts do not matter, which is why they respond to Black Lives Matter with All Lives Matter. Facts do not matter.

A Private Life shows how I found myself in some difficult times in life. We all find ourselves in hard places, but what makes America so great is there always seems to be someone with a hand reaching to pull you up from that place. My father was a selfless man who would pull over on the road to give someone in a hard place a hand. My father's generosity overwhelmed me as a kid because he had very little, but seemed very happy with sharing his last.

I ran into this homeless white couple sitting under a tree. They had everything they owned in their life with them under that tree, including their dog. The woman looked to be eight months pregnant, and her boyfriend looked like Jesus: homeless, long hair, unshaven, and dirty clothes. I went to their dog and rubbed her on the head.

They said, "Wow, Princess usually doesn't allow anyone to touch her."

I gave them $10 and began to walk away, then I turned around and told them, "I'll be back in about fifteen minutes. I can give your dog a good home. Tell me what you want for her when I get back."

When I returned, they said, "Would you give us sixty dollars, and could you continue to call her Princess?"

I said, "Deal." I opened my car door and said, "Jump in, Princess." Princess jumped in like she had known all along I was coming. I also told the couple about a church that they could go to for food and other help.

I took Princess to the vet to make sure she was okay, got her spayed, and updated her shots. Now her favorite thing is going to Del Mar Dogs Beach because she loves to swim in the ocean.

My private life did not prevent me from giving a hand to others. When I said, "I thought USC football did more for civil rights then MLK," I can honestly say they've passed the ball to the University of Missouri football team.

Leaving the Corps in the seventies was like being a runaway slave, and at that time in Southern California, no one cared less about your First Amendment Rights. The De Mau Maus was one of the many gangs in Southern California at that time. The De Mau Maus were like ISIS: niggers were always talking about beheading you if you were not black enough. Then there were the Hells Angels all over San Diego. The Crips and Bloods were also trying to claim territory back then. All kinds of shit for a young nigger to easily get caught up in when the SDPD was doing DWB stops all over San Diego.

Lucky me, I chose NASSCO after being threatened with a

beheading. The Black Panthers were needed in the sixties to stand up to the KKK. I found out firsthand in the seventies that the NAACP was worthless to the average black man. None of that shit is needed anymore. I saw, way back in the seventies, the real Black Power wasn't the NAACP: it was USC football, and now it's the University of Missouri football and their free speech, which amounts to economics.

The University of Alabama was the most racist college in the south back in the early seventies, and a lot of that had to do with George Wallace. USC is the reason their football team is integrated and making millions. That's where the real Black Power is: on and off the field.

Black Power started with bad negros with guns, ghetto niggers with attitude. The good colored folks marched and did sit-ins, while the National Association for the Advancement of Colored People was mostly ignored by Jim Crow laws. Jim Crow laws are tactics used to characterize all blacks as fried chicken and watermelon eaters who use the MF word as basic English. No one ever stood up to George Wallace until those Kennedy boys came along.

White boys played football at the best schools in the south while blacks had to go to inferior black segregated schools that are still around today and are a reminder to me of discrimination down south. The word in the hood was that Bear Bryant thought blacks were not smart enough to play quarterback for his Aryan dominance tide machine, which rolled over everyone under his control.

USC came into town with mostly black players, came in on a fucking white Trojan horse, punched that big white tide machine right between the eyes, and gave them a beat down. They whooped that ass like a stepchild. That was real Black Power. The Kennedy boys may have thrown George Wallace's ass away from the front doors of the University of Alabama, but USC kicked those doors down for black players.

It's my opinion that the USC did more for civil rights in sixty minutes on the gridiron than Martin Luther King did in sixty years marching on the streets of Dixie. We are in the 21st century and there are still white folks down in the heart of Dixie who'd rather die than accept Health Care that has anything to do with a black man (Kentucky). That's like acknowledging that Obama really is the POTUS, something they don't want to accept even on their death bed. The affluenza incumbent, Trump, has tapped into the soul of Dixie with his birtherism of Obama.

Chapter Nine
Growing Up

I believe I was between twelve and fourteen years old when I was inappropriately touched by the neighborhood dentist, Dr. Thompson. I went to have gold crowns put on a couple teeth only to find myself sedated and strapped into a chair while Dr. Thompson proceeded with his inappropriate touching. I warned him very carefully because I definitely did not want to be murdered by this freak. Look at what that freak did in The Atlanta Child Murders.

The neighborhood had all kinds of predators, and the Drag was full of dope fiends. I learned much later in life that the neighbor next door exposing herself to me was child abuse. Well, before all of that, there was a bullet wound in my right hip. I was too young to recall being shot, and definitely too young to be fighting for my life in a pit at MCRD.

After all the racist shit I had to deal with in Mobile, the Marines was where I thought I had escaped to. It was supposed to be a safe zone away from all the shit that happened in childhood. I'm almost sure I was delusional before going into the Corps, and MCRD pushed me right over the edge. My older brother had joined the Corps before I did, and I thought, if he could do it, so could I. I ignored all of his letters telling me not to join the Corps.

I guess you can pick any chapter out of A Private Life and wonder how some people survive, and others give up. It's incredible to see how many young military men are taking their lives every day. They return home from wars and see how politicians are still split along racial lines, when men of all colors have put their lives on the line to return to a nation where a racist is representing the party of Lincoln. My father did not live long enough to see our first black president, but he damn sure wouldn't like to witness all that birther shit coming out of Trump's mouth. I wish he had lived long enough to witness Barack Obama, but he would have died from seeing the treatment Obama received as the first black POTUS.

To this day, I have never been examined for my head injury at MCRD. The only thing I received from the Marine Corps was a Bad Conduct Discharge, and I'm puzzled at how I was able to make it through college and start my own business, because I could tell I had some physical and mental disabilities after coming out of the Corps.

I made it this far without any benefits from the Corps. I guess the Lord did carry me when I thought I was fighting on my own. I went from a racist, drug-infested Mobile, Alabama to a racist, drug-infested Marine Corps at MCRD and Camp Pendleton. I thought I was delusional, but I ended up on Jackrabbit Hill, where everyone was delusional, racist, and coming home from a war where the black man did not belong.

No black man should give his life for a country that treats blacks folks the way they did in the sixties, and it's not much better today, with blacks being profiled and shot down in the streets like animals. The Corps use to assault and brainwash their recruits like ISIS. Today, young people are brainwashed by the dark triad (Trump, Putin, and

Duke). The young people from Russia I invited into my home while attending school in the USA were like Trump. They had no idea that Putin had attacked the Ukraine.

Chapter Ten
Being Black

I n A Private Life, I've tried to point out the mind games the republicans and Donald Trump have mastered from Ayn Rand. Colin Kaepernick has been watching Trump profile Obama, like a lot of young black men have since Obama was elected as the first black POTUS. I'm almost sure Mr. Kaepernick has also been profiled by the police, like most black men, including Barack Obama. Most of us are profiled for DWB, which is where most of the violence begins, and usually ends with someone dead, and it's not the police. Black folks understand why Colin Kaepernick refused to stand for "The National Anthem," even if they don't agree with the way he did it.

Donald Trump comes on TV almost daily to lift up the police and demonize BLM. Donald has been doing this type of discriminating so long that he doesn't care if he's fined a thousand times. It only makes his hatred stronger, so strong that his true allegiance is more in line with Ayn Rand and the Communist Party. Mr. Trump thinks that Colin Kaepernick should move to another country. Well, I wonder if Trump should move to another country for the praise of Putin over Obama and the slap down of the generals who have put their lives on the line for his Trump Towers to stand in America.

Black folks see this man for what he is: a racist. I don't think Trump will ever see the Obama regime as being legit. We have our own saying about loose lips, which is a little different than "loose lips sinks ships." Our saying is "loose lips make a soft ass," meaning if you talk a lot of shit, someone is going to open up a can of whoop-ass on you.

Donald Trump has never had a can of whoop-ass opened up on him, which is probably the reason why he still acts like a second-grade bully. After Hillary Clinton opened up that first can of whoop-ass on Mr. Trump, hopefully he will relocate to Russia, where he praises men like Putin who shoot down commercial airliners, kill journalists, and invade countries to take their natural resources.

Oh, how times have changed. Black people have been profiled as the usual suspects for years, but now it's caught on someone's cell phone. We are not the "Real Niggers." The "Real Niggers" are these thugs and gangsters like Putin and Trump. It's been open season on black folks way too long, which has made young black men like Colin Kaepernick delusional. Can you imagine Obama acting like Donald Trump on his run to the White House? I'm having the time of my life seeing Donald Trump show the world the "Real Nigger" in America.

I'm amazed that Donald was able to con a few house niggers on his run to the Oval Office. These house niggers who hang around Trump are totally ignorant of Trump's history. I give Mike Tyson a pass for supporting Trump because he was born brain dead. Now, this doctor nigger, Ben Carson, is an enigma. He always looks like he's staring into The Twilight Zone. Where have these house niggers been for the past seven years when Trump was profiling the first black president with that birther shit to get the Tea Party and KKK riled up in a hissy fit?

I wonder if these house niggers know that Trump was sued by the federal government for housing discrimination against black folks. He won the heart of Dixie when he started profiling Obama.

We are in the 21st century. I've been delusional since the seventies, when I wore a big afro like Colin. That's too bad that Colin is seeing what I saw back in the seventies, but it's not his fight. That fight has already been fought

by Cassius Clay, John Carlos, and Tommie Smith. Black folks have already sacrificed for Colin to do what he's doing: be a black quarterback.

Chapter Eleven
The World is Shocked, Not Me

Hillary Clinton was not able to open up that first can of whoop-ass on Mr. Trump. I had a bad feeling when Bernie Sanders stayed in the fight too long. When that BLM activist and Bernie Sanders supporter Ashley Williams unfurled a cloth banner that read, "We have to bring them to heel," it was all related to that Black Youth Super Predators shit. I want to see what they, these movements (BLM and Bernie or Bust), are going to do with this closet racist, who's going to make their lives a living hell. I had my battles with a lot of these Bernie or Bust clowns here in California, but this is California. Their selfish behavior got them Trump, which will make them slaves to the plutocracy few.

These young people have fallen for the biggest con game ever. I hope they enjoy their revolution. This was not the time for apathy with young people. Once you reach the age of eighteen, you have a civic duty to be concerned with policies that make up your future. So many things had to fall into place for this con to work, and they fell into place like clockwork.

These are the things that fell into place: The economy has been weak since Bill Clinton left the White House. Donald Trump heard those cries and blamed everything on Mexicans coming across the border, taking jobs from blacks. Then there was Obamacare, which Bill Clinton trashed just weeks before the election. Then J. Comey pulled a J. Hoover in the closing days and Bernie just stayed in the fight way too long and could not reach his followers when he got out. Then a nuclear bomb was dropped on Hillary when Ashley Williams unfurled that banner, "We have to bring them to heel." I knew then that she had brought up a term that was powerful, because it related black people to dogs. It was used several times as part of Trump's march to the Oval Office.

My biggest fear came true. 46.9% of eligible voters did not vote. Colin Kaepernick was one of those who did not vote, or did a write-in, which is a delusional throw-away vote, and now we have a New Jim Crow: his name is Donald Trump. Now we have a bunch of delusional protesters marching in the streets. If you don't do your civic duty by voting, don't protest the outcome.

Chapter Twelve
The Gentrification of America

This is America, where white privilege meets the black experience. Nothing new here. Ever since 1492, Native Americans and people of color have been losing land and lives to hustlers like Donald Trump and Christopher Columbus. Columbus and his sailors pillaged and raped everything in sight, which was the real beginning of pussy grabbing. Trump is just the first president who got caught bragging about it.

Every president since George Washington grabbed pussy, which was mostly pussy of color. Columbus had a non-possessory right to use and/or enter into the property of the Native Americans with fierce violence as his uncivilized fellow sailor thugs took land. This was the beginnings of forceful easements that pushed Native Americans onto reservations all over America. Now America wants to make another easement. It wasn't enough to force them onto reservations. Now they are making more easements on the reservations with that Keystone pipeline, which will eventually destroy their water and their way of life.

Trump will grab pussy and violate the Emoluments Clause because he feels like he's above the law and courts of this land. He thinks that by appointing a judge to the Supreme Court, having Sessions as his Attorney General, and doing what Putin did to control Russia by demonizing the media is the plan he can use here. I've met so many young people from Russia who had no idea that Putin had invaded the Ukraine, or who he is killing from day to day, because they don't have a free press, which is what Trump wants: fake news.

Putin sends them on a mission and they are locked in. Igor Kornilov was making so many trips to San Clemente to the point that I thought he had found a girl up there. But I finally concluded he had instructions to take a look at San Onofre's plant. The difference between Russia and America is Freedom of the Press. While Igor was spying on San Onofre, I was spying on him and torturing him with collard greens and corn bread.

I find it amazing to see all the delusional protesters out there who did not know that Obamacare and the ACA were one and the same. They voted for Trump and thought he would have a better health care plan to replace their ACA, which is Obamacare. Obama has been in the White House for eight years now, and the republicans have been talking about something better for eight plus years now. If it were something better, it would be one of Trump's many executive orders, and it would be called Trumpcare.

Putin was looking forward to a Post West World Order with Trump. The only thing stopping the split of the Western Alliance is American patriots in our intelligence community and young patriots like the ones in that Washington State DA's office who fought against Trump's first executive order on Immigration. This is why I'm proud to be an American. I got a chance to see how those young patriots over there in that DA's office in Washington State fought for the Constitution. It's the America we don't see every day. The kind of America I'm used to is the one where General John F. Kelly of the Marines came out and proved the point I was trying to make in writing A Private Life, about the Corps and growing up black in America.

When Sgt. William E. Gugle attempted to murder me in Platoon 2115, MCRD, the base general would have done the same thing that General Kelly did: make up a lie. Tricky Dick Nixon was the commander-in-chief back then, and he was also impeached.

General Kelly was defending Donald J. Trump's latest attack on a black fallen warrior's family and a black congresswoman. Mr. Kelly was trying to defend Trump, who has done a lot worse than Tricky Nixon. Kelly is an old Marine who's just as racist as Trump. Otherwise, why would he lie on the black congresswoman and put Obama's name in his lie, something Trump does almost on a daily basis.

My commander-in-chief, Tricky Dick, was deranged. Trump is the most deranged pussy-grabbing bastard I have ever seen. If he were my commander-in-chief, he would be the second person on my hit list. Sgt. William E. Gugle would be the first. They want a race war. We had a race war in Oceanside, California. I had no response from John Conyers to my letter of what was about to go down. John was doing his thing: harassing the female help.

John Kelly attacked Gold Star Warriors of families of color, which is what these old racist Marines do. It's part of their DNA, like Trump calling black football players "sons of bitches." They don't see Puerto Ricans as Americans.

I witnessed enough in the Corps to know that General Kelly would lie for his commander-in-chief. I left Alabama as a country boy; the Marines made me an angry black man running around Jackrabbit Hill, consumed with vengeful thoughts, but I'm sure my ninth-grade history teacher and the principal over at McGill, Brother Foster, also had a role in shaping my life.

The gentrification of America is nothing more than gerrymandering and easements to take away the rights of black people. The John Kellys of the Corps are a dime a dozen, and one of them got me ready for the coming of Trump. I reached out to John Conyers right before we had a race riot in downtown Oceanside, California in 1973. Being the leader of the De Mau Maus as Songanzela, I sent a Request Mast on behalf of my Marines because John Conyers wasn't coming to the rescue.

When I got far as I could go to communicate my Marines' grievances, a one-star Marine general told me, "Stand down, Marine. You lucky you weren't hanged in Alabama."

Obama and Eric Holder are out there fighting this ongoing race war, trying to redraw some of that gerrymandering puzzle, but like I warned before Putin got into this 2016 election, we need grassroots folks to do their civic duty and vote for the progressive movement this country is ready for. When they do, look at the results. History was made with the first black POTUS. Well, history can be made again with the first black woman as governor down in Georgia, and the first Native American governor, Paulette Jordan, of Idaho's Coeur d'Alene tribe. She can be the first Native to become governor of Idaho.

Chapter Thirteen
White Slavery

In 1930 something, Willie Scott had to remove three hanging black boys from a tree on the Cuba Street property before building his house. Those boys' spirits stayed on that property as friendly ghosts. Joe Monday played games with them, and they teamed up to play tricks on me, like dropping pencils from the sky and shooting marbles from a ring.

Fast forward almost a hundred years and we may return to hanging. I mean, my base general on Camp Pendleton even told me I was lucky I wasn't hung from a tree. Millennial niggers have a lot more to worry about in America than being hung or brought to heel. If you are still one of those who think the 2016 election was about race, you are right, but you are wrong if you think Hillary Clinton is the racist. The race card was played with Trump's birther movement on the first black POTUS and with Obama responding at the 2011 White House Correspondence Dinner.

When Obama joked about Trump, I think white America did not get the jokes over there in rural Wisconsin, rural Pennsylvania, rural Michigan, and rural Ohio. They just saw the tables turned where a black man was talking down to a white man who was promising them jobs. Now they feel what black folks felt for years while being unemployed. Trump has pulled off his biggest con ever, with this promise made to the silent generation and young white men who are unemployed in rural America. They feel that their social security is not getting a cost-of-living adjustment because of the dreamers. They feel that the Obamas have taken over the White House and white lives no longer matter. They knew Donald Trump would not do any of things he promised, like jobs, because he doesn't hire Americans when he can hire foreign workers through the federal

government's H-2B visa program as cheap labor.

I think the only thing he ever made in America are those little hats that says "Make America Great Again" to con all those people who put their trust in him.

The truth is, they just did not like the idea that a black man could talk or joke about a white man. This is the silent generation, and they just wanted to be heard about White Lives Matter. This WLM group wants someone to listen to them about their COLA. with their social security. These old white people—mostly men—won, but what did they win? A white pussy-grabbing racist. When he gets in the White House, his first order of business should be to pardon Bill Cosby, because this is the New America where white slavery is now okay for Christopher Columbus and Trump to traffic in, so why not Bill Cosby? If you thought Bill Clinton should have been impeached for getting a blowjob in the White House, then you have not seen what's about to go down. The White House is about to get its first pole room. Trump will make it rain. Kanye West and Mike Tyson will be some of the first guests, and don't forget the governor of Alabama.

Obama had his basketball court. Trump will have his pole room. There will be some pussy-grabbing going on Capitol Hill. I mean, look at these old plutocrats he's considering making part of his staff.

Look at Rudy Giuliani and Newt Gingrich, another well-known pussygrabber. Clarence Thomas is another well-known sexual harasser of women and expert pussy-grabber. Pussygate is coming.

It's a close call, trying to figure out who has grabbed the most pussy out of Donald Trump and Bill Cosby, but I'm almost sure that Christopher Columbus has grabbed more pussy than both of them. White slavery is back, and this is what women have to look forward to while Trump is trying to make America great again. They can forget about trying to take this POTUS to court. He will have pussy-grabbers all the way up to the Supreme Court.

The KKK and the silent generation will continue to get screwed. Millennial niggers are used to being screwed, so it won't hurt them as bad. Social programs like social security may be reduced. The ACA, food stamps, and grants for students may be gone. That money will be tax breaks for the plutocrats. That basket of deplorables just got bigger, and there will be too many riots for that "House Nigger Sheriff David Clarke" to control. Donald Trump probably will put him in charge of hunting down young niggers like Colin Kaepernick and making them disappear, or just shooting them in the back on the streets of America for DWB.

It's a new day in America, and there will be a lot of dark, sleepless nights, the kind of nights I experienced as a kid in Alabama: black churches burning and marching in the streets. If you are one of those 46.9% who did not do your civic duty and vote, you are a hypocrite to pretend you care about women's rights, civil rights, or human rights by marching.

With Donald Trump as the POTUS, California should secede from the U.S. because Trump is not our president. California is the sixth largest economic power in the world, and was very clear about who should run this country. Clinton got 61.8% of the vote here in

California, while Trump 31.7%. Trump doesn't just have a women issue; he's a monstrous liar, a puppet for a KGB murderous thug, and should be in jail for sexual assault against many brave women. He should not be in the White House.

We are forty-eight years away from the assassination of MLK for racial inequality, and this is where we are in America. The real American carnage began with Trump's first executive order, which was to prepare for repeal of the ACA.

A voting rights case is being delayed in the Texas courts for Jeff Sessions to be elevated as Trump's Attorney General. (Sessions has a record of what he will do when elevated to that position. See the Marion Three case). We have the Women's March in Washington today, which is just the beginning of protests against Trump's idea of making America great again.

The chaos from the ACA executive order will make the market uncertain, to say the least, and this is Trump's first day in office. Trump's business international holdings and his Trump Hotel in Washington D.C. are in violation of the Constitution, and if he's not impeached, he will destroy all of Obama's work for the past eight years.

Massive crowds worldwide march against Trump. Why didn't they march to the polls (46.9% didn't vote, and now they want to protest). When you don't vote, you end up with Trump and Sessions, who want America to be "great again" by looking like Ferguson, Missouri where the slaves on the plantation did not vote. Ferguson and America are living in a state of Jim Crow laws. You cannot fail to vote, then go out in the streets and protest for something you failed to do. The civil and criminal courts have more than their share of Jim Crow sitting judges. My whole life has been one of litigation, and I know the courts are not fair. The Marion Three know the courts are not fair, and Donald Trump will make sure there will be more Jim Crow judges put there on his watch.

Pursuant to Statute, 28 U.S.C./351 et al. Rules for Judicial Conduct Proceedings, any person may file a written complaint with circuit executive concerning the actions or behavior of a judge of this court, but trying to challenge the court's decision is asking one Jim Crow judge to look at another Jim Crow judge.

This is what we are stuck with when citizens don't do their civic duty by voting. The POTUS, Donald Trump, gets to stock the courts and the Supreme Court. He's running his hotels in violation of the constitution and is the biggest pussy-grabber since Columbus.

Chapter Fourteen
Red Square

I thought Mitt Romney's assertion that Russia was America's "number one geopolitical foe" would be something that would come out the mouth of Sarah Palin, being that she can see Russia from her backyard. I still don't see Russia as a geopolitical foe, unless what Igor Kornilov told me in December of last year is true. Something about a White House MOLE. I kind of took what Igor was telling me as some James Bond shit which is why I called him Igor Kv007. Now it seems like Igor was not too far from the truth. He had my ear about Trump every day since coming to San Diego, until I put him on that red eye back to the Kremlin. He was probably fishing for orfe out of the Moskva River to go with some collard greens and corn bread, which I feel proud to have shown him how to make, since he loved them when I made them. I just don't think that orfe fish will live up to our red snapper out of the Pacific. He may also have a problem finding collard greens in Russia.

I nicknamed Igor "Jake the Snake," being that he wanted everyone to call him Jake. No one ever uses their Russian name when they come to America. He would jokingly tease some of the girls in our co-ed house by calling them the Taliban.

Putin had strict orders for Igor: he was not allowed to have fun, just do business for the Kremlin. Some of the boys invited him to go across the border to Hong Kong to play with the girls, but he was not allowed to go. Strict orders from the Kremlin.

Trump will end up firing everyone until Congress steps in and puts a stop to his madness. The whole Trump family is caught in Putin's money trap. The stories coming out of the New York Times and Washington Post are news or fake news to everyone but me. This country is headed towards a Constitution Crisis. When the oligarchs put their stamp on our 2016 election, I said, "Oh, my God." Trump will be impeached or assassinated by the oligarchs.

I would be totally surprised if Paul Manafort is not under some special protection from himself and/or the oligarchs. Manafort is as deep into Putin's money trap as Trump. I asked Igor, "How can Russia be a geopolitical foe of America when Russia cannot even compete with California from an economic standing in the world?"

Anastacia lived at my house before Igor. She was just eighteen and hated Obama because she was brainwashed and had no free press in Russia. They had the "Real Fake News," and for this POTUS to follow the marching orders of Putin instead of our intelligence agencies right here at home is treason. I understood her because I knew first-hand about brainwashing from the Corps. I finally got her to see the truth about what Russia was doing because, like Igor, she loved to eat. It took a lot of cooking and researching to prove to her that Russia was in Ukraine and that Obama wasn't the bad one she was made to believe. I started off by making her my seafood gumbo with king crabs, large shrimp, and large scallops on rice with some Mexican corn muffins.

Dominika and Igor really enjoyed my cooking, and I enjoyed them telling me how they never ate like this in Russia. Anastacia lived at my house before Igor, and she had no idea that Putin had even attacked

Ukraine. Trump did not believe that either, but for other reasons.

"It's A Small, Small World" is not just a chapter in A Private Life or a ride at Disney Land. It is a small, small world with a free press that you can call fake news until the truth is seen, which is usually the case when it's too late. With all the crazy shit that's going on in America, I try to hold on to something that is of value to me and costs nothing, like seeing how Igor all the way from Russia eating and enjoying collard greens and corn bread so much that he drank the collard greens juice from the bowl like it was a glass of grape Kool-Aid before having some of my sweet potato pie made with Courvoisier.

Vladimir terminated Igor's mission here in San Diego because he did not know how to deal with a Marine off the battlefield. He ran into the one Marine who cooked collard greens that Igor could not resist. They made him drop his guard and talk too much to the point that the Kremlin put him on a red eye flight back to Russia.

Chapter Fifteen
Espionage

The commander-in-chief has been in office for less than two months, but there has been a dossier on his every move well before he even imagined he would be taking the oath to be the POTUS, an oath which he violates every day with a different lie. I think this speaks volumes about the people who put him in the White House. They either don't care about his lies or believe them. Either way, it makes them part of this basket of deplorables.

Oh, how the times have changed. Spy Craft Tools and WikiLeaks have put a mole in every smartphone and television set around the world's cyberspace. Putin has weaponized Trojans and viruses to attack us in 2017, according to one of my Russian roommates, Igor Kv007, aka Jake the Double Agent.

Jake came to San Diego as a good Russian spy, but like a good Marine, I broke his will with my collard greens, corn bread, and sweet potato pie. Jake joked about how Trump got punked when he was in Russia. Putin demanded Jake to return to the Kremlin in the middle of night. He asked me to take him to the airport to jump on a red eye flight. Jake the Snake. That Russian boy loved drinking the juice from my collard greens.

What Russia needs is some black folks over there who know how to cook collard greens, because if Jake's comrades like collard greens the way he does, I can solve all of this new atomic bomb (information warfare) talk with a bowl of collard greens and corn bread. Black folks have been profiled as the usual suspects for years, only to use the smartphone to show how they have really been railroaded for years (see the Justice Department's findings for Ferguson, Missouri). Black folks have been hung from trees, put in jail cells, and murdered for years by America's Jim Crow laws, until DNA and technology intelligence put a temporary stop to a lot of this madness. It had been open season on black folks for way too long. Black folks go to jail for years for rock cocaine. White folks do no time for powdered cocaine.

Can you imagine Obama acting like Donald Trump on his run to the White House? I'm having the time of my life seeing Donald Trump show the world the "Real Nigger" in America, and Obama the more honorable man. I'm amazed that Donald was able to con a few house niggers on his run to the Oval Office. These house niggers who hang around Trump are totally ignorant of Trump's history. I give Mike Tyson a pass for supporting Trump because he was born brain dead. Now, Kanye West and this doctor nigger, Ben Carson, are true enigmas. Carson always looks like he's staring into The Twilight Zone. I guess that's why he thought slaves were immigrants.

Where have these house niggers been for the past seven years when Trump was profiling the first black president with that birther shit? White folks were so caught up on the name "Obamacare." That's the reason they were so easily conned.

I can only use the layman's terms for how I see Trump. I would need DSM-5 to come up with new terms, but his whole administration is a bunch of liars. Gen. Flynn is a liar. Sessions lied in his Congressional Confirmation Hearing, and Trump is a compulsive liar. Patriots from the intelligence community should be given protection where they can be classified as PATRIOTS instead of leakers.

Look at us now with this idiot POTUS and all of his Russian spies. Trump has received hundreds of millions of dollars from the Russians on deals that are worthless to the Russians. There's a bigger picture coming into focus for Putin. If Congress subpoenaed Trump's tax returns starting around 1990 to now, they would have all the evidence they needed to impeach Mr. Trump.

But this is America, where the republicans play these juvenile games like their juvenile president, tweeting shit that has nothing to do with being the POTUS. I can't be the only one seeing this guy for what he is: a stone-cold, crazy con man, tweeting crazy shit about Obama wiretapping his Trump Hotel, and the ongoing tweet fights with Arnold Schwarzenegger.

The only thing keeping him from being taken from the White House in a white straitjacket is a biased Congress that gets him to sign executive orders every day, destroying Obama's legacy. They envy the idea that Obama did it all with a Do-Nothing Congress for eight years, and they deeply regret that Obama was able to break up their all-white boy clubs since GW, so much so that their constituents elected this pussy-grabbing racist profiler to the highest office in the free world. They will defend the indefensible until he's removed in a straitjacket, hopefully before the Apocalypse. The football is in his hand, and he's just one tweet away from fumbling.

Chapter Sixteen
The Color of Authority, Part II

All the people who feel stressed by this so-called POTUS's constant lies, discrimination, and vile bigotry should get used to it until he is impeached or replaced by the people. He's only fulfilling his promises. He conned his way into the White House with his reckless abandon of lies. He's a fraud. He had no better healthcare plan that he promised the people. It was a lie. He expected Congress to have a plan.

He still owes thousands of people, who have done work for him and have never gotten paid a fair price for their labor. He owes the people of America an apology for promising to bring jobs back home from overseas when he petitions the government each year to hire people from other countries for his Trump Mar-a-Lago estate, instead of people right here in America. Everything he makes is made overseas.

He owes black people an apology for the emotional toll of profiling the first black POTUS, and his cowardly acts of constantly attacking Obama. I'm guessing he continues his discrimination as the POTUS in salute to his dad, Fred, who took on the federal government in his housing discrimination against black people.

He owes white people an apology for promising them the moon and stars, and if you are still a believer, I hope you come to your senses soon, because this man cares about no one but himself. If it means taking healthcare from 22 million people who are mostly white, he will do it in a heartbeat unless Congress stops him. He will fire anyone who gets in his way unless Congress stops him. His Color of Authority is to destroy anyone who's not loyal to him and his drive to turn back the hands of time.

One of my newest guests in my home schooled me on Trump, The Twin Towers, and rap. First, he's a young white boy with no college who spent a lot of his youth listening to rap. He's from Indiana and tells me that a lot of his friends are like him and voted for Trump because they want to make the fast buck, like Trump, and don't care who they hurt to get it, like Trump.

I asked him about the Twin Towers and he said, "They blew up the Twin Towers to get to the gold under the Twin Towers."

I said, "You are in California now, and when you talk that conspiracy shit like that, it's called 'being out on a limb.' Shirley MacLaine will tell you, 'Young man, get your ass off that limb.' " This kid was telling me about some recycled Trump retweet shit like that wild conspiracy shit he retweeted, accusing Hillary Clinton of Murder. He told me they are more likely to believe in Donald Trump's retweets and rap than what they are teaching in school about government.

He says a lot of white kids like himself prefer to believe this way. I asked him if he believed in the Constitution of the United States of America. He said, "Too hard."

I told him when rappers say crazy shit like, "Why did Bush bring down the Towers?" It's just conspiracy bullshit rhymes.

So usually when he tells me things that don't make sense, I tell him. "All right, young man. Get your ass off that limb."

Trump knows nothing about government, and that's just the way they like him. I asked him about all of the people who may lose their healthcare because of Trump. He said, "Young people like myself don't care who we hurt to get ahead, like Trump. We live for today and don't care about tomorrow."

This attitude is the new attitude of young white boys, which is the Donald Trump brand, coded "America First" for the White Nationalist Movement. You have people in the White House like Sebastian Gorka and Steve Bannon and wonder why we are shocked by the new America looking like the streets of Germany in the 1930s and the Russians running around Red Square saying, "S Novim Godom" in September. Putin's money didn't just buy Trump; it made downpayments through Facebook, Twitter, and any other social media space where they could lay their foundation for their cyberspace warfare.

Igor Kornilov was right. We are at war with Russia, and Trump should be hung for treason. Trump is a compulsive liar. Patriots from the intelligence community should be given protection where they can be classified as PATRIOTS instead of leakers. Look at us now with this idiot POTUS and all of his Russian spies. Trump has received hundreds of millions of dollars from the Russians on deals that are worthless to the Russians. There's a bigger picture coming into focus for Putin. If a special counsel subpoenaed The Trump Organization LLC for their taxes from around 1990 to present, they would have all the evidence they needed to impeach Mr. Trump.

But this is America, where the republicans in Congress play these juvenile games like their juvenile president, tweeting shit that has nothing to do with being the POTUS.

Trump once said, "There's nothing wrong with Putin being a murderer."

I'm willing to bet that the mob has murdered a lot in the name of Trump, and buried the bodies probably right under his Towers where he sleeps. No one but the Devil can sleep on top of souls.

Trump doesn't think about life. He's no better than the thugs who murder each other in the ghetto. Trump thinks he's entitled and untouchable, and people like that usually end up in an orange jumpsuit. Trump picked his Treasury Secretary, Mnuchin, probably because he foreclosed on 36,000 people and made them homeless. Steven Mnuchin is one who thinks he's entitled, too. Mnuchin's wife, Louise Linton, got to ride around on taxpayer's airplanes and talk about all the brand-name shit they were wearing from making citizens homeless.

Trump and his administration have no problem taking 22 million people's healthcare insurance away from them, which would kill thousands of people every year just to give a tax break to the rich. They have no problem taking people's homes and putting them out on the streets, making them homeless. What happened to basic humanity with these people who think they are entitled to shit on gold toilets while others live on the streets?

I have known for years that our Jim Crow legal system is racist, starting with the Supreme Court, and now the Trump pardon of Sheriff Joe Arpaio. Trump will obstruct justice for as long as it takes to make sure his family and supporters are not charged with crimes. Do we have a "Constitutional Crisis" or what? The closer they look at the hacking that took place in the 2016 election, the more I feel cheated by Trump and the Russians.

Robert E. Lee chose the Confederacy over the Union, which was treason. Trump chose Russia over the USA to attack our country in cyberwarfare which should also be treason. He should hang, because the Russians will not stop hacking our systems. Trump will continue to turn his back because he benefitted from this cyberwarfare and prefers to do nothing because of his connections to Russia.

Igor verified that dossier even before it was news in America. Anastacia lived at my house before Igor. She was just eighteen and hated Obama because she was brainwashed and had no free press in Russia. They had the "Real Fake News," and for this POTUS to follow the marching orders of Putin instead of our intelligence agencies right here at home is treason.

I understood her because I knew first-hand about brainwashing from the Corps. I finally got her to see the truth about what Russia was doing because, like Igor, she loved to eat. It took a lot of cooking and researching to prove to her that Russia was in Ukraine and that Obama wasn't the bad one she was made to believe.

I had a bigger challenge with Igor because his mission was different from Anastacia's. His was the San Onofre Nuclear plant.

I started off by making Anastacia my seafood gumbo with king crabs, large shrimp, and large scallops on rice with some Mexican corn muffins. Anastacia and Igor really enjoyed my cooking, and I enjoyed them telling me how they never ate like that in Russia.

Anastacia lived at my house before Igor, and she had no idea that Putin had even attacked Ukraine. Trump did not believe that either, but for other reasons. "It's A Small, Small World" is not just a chapter in A Private Life or a ride at Disney Land. It is a small, small world with a free press that you can call fake news until the truth is seen, which is usually the case when it's too late.

With all the crazy shit that's going on in America, I try to hold on to something that is of value to me and costs nothing, like seeing how Igor all the way from Russia eating and enjoying collard greens and corn bread so much that he drank the collard greens juice from the bowl like it was a glass of grape Kool-Aid before having some of my sweet potato pie made with Courvoisier.

Vladimir terminated Igor's mission here in San Diego because he did not know how to deal with a Marine off the battlefield. He ran into the one Marine who used collard greens instead of waterboarding to get actionable information from him.

I think about all the stories that came from waterboarding. One in particular was from a KSM that claimed some black Muslims in Montana had planned to wage jihad in America. There are no fucking black folks in Montana. Maybe two or three. And how stupid does Facebook have to be to get caught up in espionage with the Russians? I guess only Facebook knows the cost of being a capitalist whore. Only Facebook knows the real cost. The Russians paid them blood money to commit espionage. Facebook got the money at a cost that elected Trump, who feels like he wakes up every day in a money box in America.

I remember seeing a game show where they put you in this big glass box and turned on a machine that blew money all over inside the glass box. Whatever you could grab was yours. That's how Trump and Zuckerberg feel, as if someone put them in a big moneybox and turned on the machine.

This man has split this nation every day he's been in office. On his 257th day, he threw paper towels at the Puerto Ricans like it was some kind of game when people were dying in Puerto Rico. They should have thrown one of those rolls of cheap ass towels back at his dumbass, like the shoe throwing at Bush in Iraq.

This reality TV clown is so much dumber than Bush. The division he has caused this country is incredible. Who is he to complain about black football players kneeling because of police killing black men in the streets of America every week under the American Flag and going to Jim Crow courts where they are being found not guilty under the American flag?

Of course we are not going to stand for a flag that still treats us differently from everybody else. That's why this BLM movement got on a fast track. Mark Zuckerberg made a lot of money from Russian troll farms and helped get Donald Trump elected POTUS. If he did that in Russia, trying to get someone to replace Putin, where would he be right now? In an Orenburg jail cell.

If Mark didn't want America to be like Russia, and he believed in democracy and Justice, he would stop hiding behind the 1st and 5th Amendments and stop playing this espionage game with Putin. I know this is a thin line because anyone should be able to make money from anywhere, but not at the cost of losing the freedoms that protect you: the Constitution (1st and 5th Amendments in his case).

Chapter Seventeen
This Is America

Here stands this trailer trash white man, standing only because of Putin's blood money, who had no problem expressing sexual feeling about his own daughter, Ivanka, on Howard Stern.

This is America. Here stands this white man who confessed on live TV to being a pussy-grabber.

This is America. Here stands this white man who profiled the first black POTUS with his made-up birther lies.

This is America. Here stands a white man who lies every day, and has told more than three thousand lies since being elected to the highest office in the land.

This is America. Here stands a white man who holds an office that I knew would turn his life upside down.

This is America. Here stands a white man who created a lie like Spygate, a scorched earth strategy that would require not just this white man, but many white men from the House and House Speaker Paul Ryan to pull it off.

This is America. Spygate would be the end of life as we once knew it. It would be the beginning of a Constitutional crisis in this childish Gambino America where only this white man and white men like him, such as Speaker Ryan, can get away with lying.

This is America.

This is America, where there will always be a dysfunctional basket of deplorables who buy Trump's deep state BS year after year. They are so dysfunctional that they will forget how House Speaker Ryan visited a Harley plant in Wisconsin and said, "Tax reform can put American manufacturers and American companies like Harley-Davidson on a much better footing to compete in the global economy and keep jobs in America." It was a bunch of objectivism deep state BS lies. Associate Justice of the Supreme Court, Clarence Thomas, has always been a nigger, and it has nothing to do with the tone of his skin and more to do with the tone of his character. The characters of Donald Trump, Christopher Columbus, and Paul Ryan are that of a nigger. The "Real Niggers" of America. Paul Ryan graduated from his white lies about "misstated marathon times" and "the intense P90X workouts" to allowing U.S. Representative Devin Nunes create wiretapping lies against Obama. Ryan was also the author of a tax bill for the very rich, and now he's allowing Trump to tell this super lie, Spygate.

This is America, where only a white man can profile a real president as being illegitimate at fighting for his own legitimacy.

Paul Ryan and Devin Nunes are playing a dangerous game of treason. Paul Ryan was known as the man with all the right numbers to bring the debt ceiling under control, but in the end, it was only a con game to get his tax bill on Trump's desk. It all makes a lot of sense now that Paul Ryan used his reading of Ayn Rand's books to turn the table on those at Harley-Davidson and the nation. He saw Trumpism in Atlas Shrugged before there was this character of Trump, who cares nothing about this country and would turn to a scorched earth strategy to save his own ass.

This is America. Trump's strategy did not begin with Spygate. It's been going on since he's been in office in violation of the Emoluments Clause. He's been stealing from Americans every day since his election and standing up for police abusing their power.

This is his America. Trayvon Martin, Sanford, Florida. Verdict: Not guilty.

This is America. Eric Garner, New York.
This is America. Freddie Gray, Baltimore.
This is America. Sam Dubose, Cincinnati.
This is America. Philando Castile, St. Anthony.
This is America. Terence Crutcher, Oklahoma. Verdict: Not Guilty.
This is America. Alton Sterling, Baton Rouge.
This is America. Jamar Clark, Minneapolis.
This is America. Jeremy McDole, Wilmington.
This is America. William Chapman II, Portsmouth.
This is America. Walter Scott, North Charleston.
This is America. Eric Harris, Tulsa.
This is America. Tamir Rice, Cleveland.
This is America. Akai Gurley, New York.
This is America. Michael Brown, Ferguson.
This is America.

These killings of black folks is America. This is America, where there's a George Floyd every week in a different name. I have PTSD from growing up black in America.

Chapter Eighteen
Democracy In Distress

These people were willing to go to jail for Donald Trump, William Barr, Mike Pence, Mike Pompeo, and Michael Flynn; he cannot pardon them all. Trump followers only have five senses; Trump has six, with his sixth sense being a reptilian survival sense, as in 666, Lucifer. Robert Mueller was making some progress with Michael Flynn until Barr stepped in and now what you have is a complicit government at the expense of Ukraine being taken back by Russia. Flynn, Trump, and his family are all swimming in the Swamp Waters of Treason. The Red Square chapter where my friend, Igor Kornilov, outed Trump years ago as being the Mole in the White House. Finally, I believe Mueller and Judge Emmet Sullivan hearing the Flynn case had gotten close to getting Flynn to turn over on Trump until Barr put a stop to the investigation. William Barr is the main clog in this public corruption case of obstruction of justice with money from the Russian mob, Dmytro Firtash. Lucifer was given a new weapon to play with that killed a lot of black people. WAKE UP young Black people and take COVID-19 seriously because it's killing us quicker than anyone else. The Black Kids on Daytona Beach streets yesterday was more Black on Black crimes because that Covid-19 is peaking down there and with no social distancing or mask wearing, it was a shocking scene. They were there for the Memorial Day weekend. WHAT KILLS BLACK PEOPLE MORE besides other Black people? COVID-19. They are there partying and could return home sick and if it doesn't kill them, it may kill someone they love, I guess a million souls in the ground, including Herman Cain was not a wakeup call and Black people just keep dying. Black people will just keep dying in great numbers that has been going on well before Covid-19. This Commander in Chief fired the Pandemic Team in 2018 and has been defunding the Centers for Disease Control, his refusal to use the Defense Production Act and let the Federal Government take charge has put First Responders and this Country in a horrible Hell (see IHHMEProjection) for your City and State.

This POTUS, Georgia Governor Kemp and that wokeness Florida Governor is knowingly killing folks (particularly Blacks and old folks) and Alabama has ran out of ICU beds in the whole State and I recall Alabama Governor saying we are not California, New York City, well you may be worse, time will tell because they were all down on the beach in Alabama too over the weekend and one young White boy said, "If he's not going to wear Mask, I'm not going to wear Mask" the reporter ask 'who are you talking about, the President" he replied, "Yes Mam." These Governors down South is killing all of these Black people and Trump hasn't missed a beat in trying to take away Obamacare These young Black people that was on the streets of Daytona Beach, Florida yesterday makes the whole Black race look bad and I pray that First Responders don't have to risk their lives to save them if they get sick with Covid-19. If those White people down on the beach in Alabama want to follow Trump to hell, then I don't want to chastise them. I just feel that Black people should be more aware because the statistics don't lie and it takes approximately 3 days to get sick, which is time to give it to your parents, grandparents, and other innocent people. This is 2024, isn't it? Why TF are black people still fighting for their voting rights? that life-threatening incident in Platoon 2115 when I was 17 years old and less than a week at MCRD. William E. Gugle gave me something that Alabama was unable to do, and Jackrabbit Hill and Tom Metzer gift wrapped it for me on 4th of July 1973. William E. Gugle and Tom Metzer had no psychological composure or moral compass, and it was bad timing for me to be joining the Corps with these two men playing a role in young men's lives, and it damn sure did not help that the 2nd Battalion, 5th Marines, was returning back to Jack Rabbit Hill from Viet Nam. I found a place on Jackrabbit Hill that I've been trying to run away from all my life in Alabama. Clarence Thomas and Samuel Alito have really put their hands on the scales of justice, and it has X, Z, and Alpha grievance shots to hell. They are in some of the best schools I only dream about getting into; they could have run to the war; that's what I did; I ran to the war. They are blaming everyone but themselves for not running to the war. I want to get up and do something about our world, but I'm not getting around like I used to these days. I would have loved to be given the chance to get into UCLA, where my daddy brothers (Carmen and Walter) went to school. I mean, the movie stars even have a hard time getting their kids into those schools, but with the money they have, they usually get their kids in. I had been following Trump since I was a kid and got to see up close and personal who Trump was through his books and businesses that he had gotten into, only to bankrupt them and find different tax holes he could squib through. I was born in madness—the assassinations of JFK, Robert, and MLK Jr., the Vietnam War, and Watergate. Trump found a way to put all this madness on steroids.

Trump knows there is no "good side" in the Israel-Palestine conflict, so he stays on the sideline. There's no difference between Israel and the USA; they are both occupiers. If we don't learn from history, we allow innocent people to be born into hate. My ninth-grade history teacher made sure I understood that MLK Jr. was a communist, I met a lot of communist and MLK Jr. was no communist.; one of the last communists I met almost lost his hand to my pit bull, Cal, or, like my girlfriend likes to call him, Biggie. We should all know about Project 2025, America's Dark Future. Trump's transition project if re-elected. His MAGA followers like to call it their Republic, that supposedly replaces our Democracy. Putin's last spy was sent to the house around 2014, give or take a few years. Putin sent him down before Igor and Anastacia arrived. Cal was a pretty good judge of these communists coming over from Russia.

159

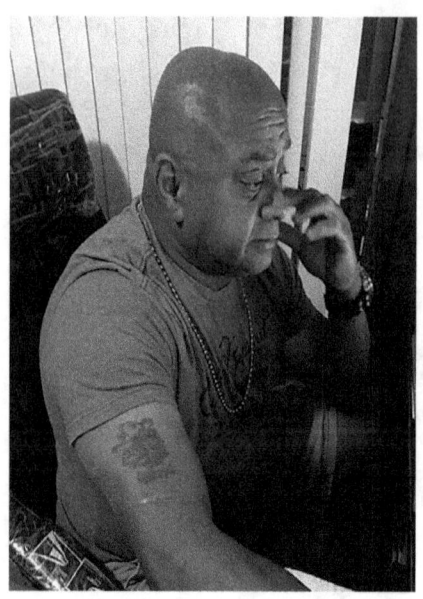

Chase Hayes, while working on the book   151 Mutt Jeep

Just another day in the Corps. My office is set on a hill less than a football field away from the rifle range. I had just logged 0300 on my duty sheet after making my rounds on Jackrabbit Hill. Before I could open the door to my office, I heard this loud blast down on the range. I jumped into my old 151 Mutt and made sure I had an extra clip for my Glock. When I got to the range, I saw Burns standing over the body of another Marine with a shotgun. I stood behind my Mutt with my Glock aimed center mass at him and convinced him to put the shotgun into the trunk of his car and go out the back gate of Camp Pendleton, where I had called in reinforcements to take him down there. One Marine was dead, and I could have won the shootout because my Mutt would have taken most of his buck shots and I would have emptied my Glock on him. The Division Commander, Major Gould, thought that I should have emptied my Glock into him on the spot, so he relieved me of my gun and told me to clock out. That's not my job to kill another black marine; we have a UCMJ; that was their job. I thought I would be going back to the Brig for not taking Burns down, but I didn't know what happened down on that range with all the racial shit going on up on the hill.

I definitely thought that I would not be allowed to play football and put back in the Brig. I was only in the Corps trying to get school benefits to get into college and walk on somewhere like USC, but after the Corps and my BCD, my chances were already slim. Now I knew I had no chance whatsoever because at that time, kids with perfect records were paying to get into USC by rich parents and having people take their SAT's and help them with all of their classes. I really fell in love with USC but hated LA; it was too big for a country boy. It really took me back to McGill, where I had to pick up trash after school just to be there and was unable to play football. It seemed like I had to always work and not be able to be a full-time student. I went back to building ships in San Diego while going to Evening College and got an AA before enrolling at SDSU. I recall not having any of the textbooks for the classes I was taking and just having to listen to the professor.

I was basically taking classes and not being able to read the textbook assignments given out by the professor. I did this with some of my classes at San Diego City and Mesa, but it wasn't working that well at State. I had a young family, and they were my priority like when I was 14 and had to build ships and work after school. Big Baby had a lot more talent than I had, and he did not make it to the NFL. I felt I had to do everything that I could to be one of those who got out of Mobile and beat the odds. I'm sure my GPA took a hit at State for not having all of my books; used books cost almost as much as new books. I applied to UCSD graduate school before even petitioning for my BA from State and began to wonder how I was doing this with not a lot of money. I had to get some fast money, so I opened a boutique, Mischievous Cliche, selling only Juco designer clothes, mostly designer jeans, which I got at off-price, cost on terms, sometimes at net 60 (two-month loans were like free money), and I was making so much money that I was hanging out in the same clubs that all the Chargers were hanging out in.

Junior Seau was one of the Chargers that I kept running into at some of my hangouts, and they had made it to the NFL but never seemed happy. With football came head injuries and tearing up your knees every year. I have had several ACL and meniscus tears, and I got all of that in the Corps—the head injury at MCRD and knee injuries playing football (two years for the Marine Corps). I had it all, which creates all kinds of things but peace in America, where in 2024 every Republican candidate still thinks the Civil War was over state rights instead of slavery and the South is still the South. Progressive blacks are one of the reasons why Trump even got into office, and if they don't go to the polls in 2024, they might not ever be able to talk about voting rights again if we don't have a democracy.

What I've Learned Through My Experience

The day I was assaulted in Platoon 2115 by Sgt. William E. Gugle was the day I checked out of the Marines mentally. I was left unconscious in a mud pit, bleeding from the head, mouth, and ears, and dying from being hit blindsided with the butt of my M-14 rifle while doing bends and thrusts. I felt disappointment and confusion. I was barely eighteen and lay there in my own blood from noon chow to sunset, and was carried to my bunk by other Marines, never being able to go to the hospital or seek medical help. I had to hold in my anger and rage because Sgt. Gugle had already killed one Marine in a pool and had injured other Marines in MCRD Platoon 2115.

The rest of my time in the Marines was spent in hatred, confusion, rage, and anger. Hatred of Sgt. William E. Gugle. Hatred of the Marines. Confusion from a head injury and not really knowing where I was from time to time, until I was sent to Fort Leavenworth for petty theft and disorderly conduct, as well as breaking into the base NCO club and destroying all the machines. Hatred for being court martialed with an all-white jury, all old, white officers.

I left MCRD in a fog and had no discipline about what I was doing in the Corps. The 2nd Battalion 5th Marines returned back to Jackrabbit Hill from Vietnam with a lot of their own hatred for going all the way to Vietnam only be told by the Vietnamese to, "Go home. This is not your war. Your war is in America."

Those Marines had race issues that only made things worse. My rage grew upon Jackrabbit Hill, Camp Pendleton, the Margarita Area, area 33, because it was home to the KKK and the black Marines returning home from Vietnam. This was not the Marines the recruiting office sold to me prior to enlisting. The black Marines formed a group in Nam called the De Mau Maus, a name they got from an Africa gang. It was solely for protection. They feared they would be killed by another white Marine over in Vietnam and needed to protect each other. They named me *Songanzela* and told me it means "to guide," and they wanted me to go on a "Request Mast."

Don't exclude yourself from this life. Be present. Even if someone sometimes was not there for you. Be there for yourself. You're AMAZING, and no one can take that away from you. Some of the happiest times in my life was getting out some of the complaints to the commanding general.

To this day and time, I have never been examined for my head injury at MCRD. The only thing I received from the Marine Corps was a bad conduct discharge, and I'm puzzled how I was able to make it through college and start my own business, because I could tell that I had some physical and mental disabilities coming out of the Corps. I made it this far without any benefits from the Corps. I guess the Lord did carry me when I thought I was walking on my own.

I went from a racist, drug-infested Mobile, Alabama to a racist, drug-infested U.S. Marine Corps at MCRD and Camp Pendleton. I thought I was delusional when I ended up on Jackrabbit Hill with my head injury, but everyone was delusional, racist, and coming home from a war where the black man did not belong.

No black man should give his life for a country that treats blacks the way they did in the sixties, and it's not much better today, with blacks being profiled and shot down in the streets like animals. My first week out of the Corps, San Diego Chief of Police, Bill Kolender, told me blacks were born to be profiled.

I grew up in a world that has been a battlefield to survive since childhood, in a home where I had to be enough for my family to survive. I survived childhood, and survived the Marine Corps, where I was never enough. I was only liked when I played football for the

Corps. I survived an attempted murder on my life during my first week at MCRD, and survived racism. Survived America. I gave the Marine Corps everything I had except my soul and my deuce and a quarter. They gave me my life back, which has a new title to it now, not honorable but dishonorable, a BCD (bad conduct discharge) for standing up for those who couldn't stand up for themselves. I survived the Corps and driving around San Diego with other young black Marines, living our lives until we were profiled like runaway slaves.

When Obama was elected, I thought about writing him about a pardon, but I felt like someone would think I was using the race card now that there's a black president in office. Well, I did not want to use him as some kind of advantage, but I do remember writing the Secretary of the Navy and getting a letter from him saying if I would have detailed everything at my Court Martial, it probably would have made a difference back then. When I read his letter, I thought I wasn't able to explain anything back then because of my state of mind. I just remember Sgt. Gugle saying, "Good Marines never talk about what happens to anyone in basic training," So I never did talk about it. I only wanted to be a good Marine. I was one of those few good men. Brainwashed.

I did not say anything in my Court Martial or for years after I got out of the Corps. I was profiled at McGill-Toolen, by the Corps, and many times by the SDPD, where Chief Kolender believes, "Blacks are born to be profiled." In 2020, there's still so much "good trouble" left in this world.

W

Closing

The shooting of Trayvon Martin, the kid in Sanford, Florida by the neighborhood watch is a sad reminder of what happened to my youngest brother, Earl, in a small town in Texas.

Earl was born on Christmas day. He had moved to Texas to be around family, who had relocated there from Mobile. Mike tried to reconstruct the incident in a telephone conversation. It boiled down to the police making way too many decisions based on their judgment alone, which they are not always equipped to do. It's been my personal experience that the police are more biased in rendering judgment or "care," in my brother's case, against anyone who's black before doing a thorough investigation. My brother, according to Mike, was pulled over for drunk driving. His slurred speech was taken by the police as being intoxicated. He had a brain aneurysm that needed medical attention immediately. He was locked-up in a Texas small town cell for days. How many days does it take to figure out if a person is sick and not drunk?

He later died from that condition because medical attention was not given in a timely manner. My heart is broken. It cracks every time I hear how young black men are treated.

We have gone from hanging young black men to shooting them down in the streets like prey. The Sanford shooting is sadly just one of many instances of black boys being murdered in this country every year because of racial profiling.

There are ongoing FBI investigations into some missing black men in Georgia that point directly to an old white rogue cop in a small town in Georgia. I had a fear of cops in Mississippi when I was as young as fifteen. My heart is broken again over the shooting of another black kid.

In the Sanford shooting, he was a kid going home with candy and a soda. I'm angry about how many cover-ups take place in little police stations all over this country. I have heard the Sanford story a thousand times. The kid died because he was racially profiled. He died for being black. He was hunted down like prey, then left in a cold room for three days like an animal. This is nothing new to black men.

I'm lucky to be alive today, twenty years after they pulled Emmett's body from the Tallahatchie River. After my discharge from the Corps, I was traveling through Mississippi with family members. We stopped at a place for breakfast. I was friendly with a white waitress and a group of white boys made threats towards me. I guess I should consider myself lucky I don't live down there because my MOS is to protect myself by any means necessary.

Back then, I didn't know Emmett's story. I do know the top G-man was an abject racist, fascist, and a general bigot. He coupled that with his omnipotent power, which he wielded like a lightsaber to further his selfish, paranoid, corrupted agenda, which included destroying the character of MLK and Jack. I had a 9mm stuck in my face just for taking out my trash one morning in San Diego. I've stopped counting the number of times I've been pulled over for "DWB."

Racism is not a disease; it's a natural sin that started with hatred for slaves. Slaves passed being the object of that hatred on to coloreds. Coloreds passed it on to negros. Negros passed it on to blacks. Blacks passed it on to the black kid in Sanford, who was an all-American kid. The sin should end here with the Sanford murder. Sadly, it will not. The Sanford incident is something black men have experienced way too often in America. And they call us the angry black man.

Yes, I'm angry over the Sanford murder. I'm angry over the senseless death of my brother. I'm angry over all the black-on-black crime. I'm angry over rogue cops getting away with killing young black men, which seems almost daily. My neighbor, who shouted, "Someone should take a gun and blow Obama's brains out," his anger was based on hate.

I grew up in this kind of hate, where the Klan was ravaging neighborhoods in the name of the Bible. Jack's, Robert's, and MLK's deaths were all hate crimes. The KKK was like what the terrorists are doing under the name of the Qur'an.

Things that should not have happened to begin with quickly become too complicated, like ISIS. ISIS is nothing more than remnants left over from the catastrophe of the "Shock and Awe" launch on Iraq.

I don't want to think I'm blessed because I survived a lot of hate. That's some bullshit, Christians probably would tell me. The KKK were so-called Christians, but they were the ISIS of the sixties to black folks, mostly in the south. There were hangings into the late sixties.

I have no delusions about fiction and science. The Bible is fiction. The Bible says, "Slaves, obey your master," which made niggers submissive and helped shape Jim Crow laws. As a black man, I don't feel blessed. Maybe lucky to be alive. I could have taken the bullet from one-eyed Jack, like a lot of innocent kids do every year in the black ghettos of America. I could have taken Chico's bullet, or Private Psycho's bullet. I lost most of my innocence when I was left for dead in that mud pit at MCRD.

I could have stayed in Alabama if I wanted that type of Marine Corps bullshit treatment. I lost my lighthouse—my dad, Earl—and a few Marines up on Jackrabbit Hill who were looking for a better life, like myself.

Don't look to the courts or politics for that better life. The courts are twisted with Ayn Rand tactics. You can call them Jim Crow courts or

Ayn Rand courts. Politicians and lawyers have studied this objectivism for years, which is simply turning the truth to fit a certain narrative. My studies have been in psychology, but my hobby has been our Jim Crow courts, where I have been labeled a vexatious litigant because of my pro se status, which has more to do with class and not the actual law. I could not be a good lawyer because I have a conscience. I would be a Roman J. Israel, Esq. litigator.

It makes a big difference in America when you have money. Do you know how many poor blacks are in prison for admitting to crimes they did not do because they had pro bono representation? Well, O.J. is not one of them, and if he had not been rich, he would be on California's death row.

These Ayn Rand philosophies are from the hell pits of Russia, and Trump appointing hundreds of District Court Jim Crow judges just made the system worse. The perfect example of using an Ayn Rand tactic is what those Republican politicians did with the Trump-Russia dossier, where they twisted the truth to fit their narrative and made Christopher Steele the target.

This is the system we live in, and this is the end of my journey. I'm glad I made law a hobby and not a career. My action against the Corps has been mostly administrative, and I do have an action pending in the 9th Circuit Appellate courts: Hayes vs NASSCO.

There's mostly discrimination in America. But now that you know what it's like to walk in my shoes, I have a question for you: Do you think we live in a post-racial America when white cops get away with murdering black men weekly in these Jim Crow courts and the president tries to turn the tables and make black football players the target? I do not think we live in a post-racial America, and I don't know if I'm blessed or cursed, but I do know that no one should have to grow up being the target of hate in America.

A Letter to My Angel

Mary Scott (Momma)

Dear Momma,

The hardest chapter to write about is the one you don't write about. Mike told me her first child was a child of rape and Nanny wanted her to put him up for adoption, which makes a lot of sense now being that Nanny never like talking about anything. Mike only told me about her rape in these last two years of her life. I was shocked but it answered some things I saw in the dysfunction of our family, her first born formed the nucleus of the family and the genetic drift I fought with my whole life until I spoke with Dr. Sieber about it along with my experience in the Corps. This rage was part of my childhood life and I couldn't hold back not a second longer because it was eating me alive; but once I got it out, his response was like he believes in critical race theory and that black lives didn't matter to him, my primary, Dr. Osborne had been my primary for almost 20 years and I thought he had made a good choice for me, no, this guy refused to read my memoir or learn anything about my past, my black experience, black lives did not matter to him. He was one of those people with critical race theory when it came to history and the years on years it take to become dysfunctional in America.

What has it all been for? Blacks dying in the street like prey, and we always knew the real terrorist was right here in America. I knew that before I joined the Marines, only to find out that you can't run away from them in Alabama, and they were not in Vietnam, but right there on Jackrabbit Hill in Camp Pendleton, California. William E. Gugle sounded that alarm at MCRD, where the KKK in the Corps outnumber regular Marines and continues to grow, as what the world witnessed this past January 6 on the capital.

In the end, we need to ask ourselves, "Did Obama kill Bin Laden, or in death, did Bin Laden kill democracy through Trumpism? I knew of Q when it was in its infancy days, when this young white boy, Andrew Phillip Stevens, told me Bush knocked down the towers. After arguing with him for hours that those were only Jadakiss lyrics, I gave up. As crazy as it seemed back then, it has a way of having some truth to it today, if you put the whole puzzle together involving Bin Laden, Mullah, and Trump.

My Life's Darkest Chapter

(Sgt. William E. Gugle all the way to the far right)

To go from smart, gifted, and a star CYO football player for the Almighty Heart of Mary Lions to almost dying in a freaking MCRD boot camp from a cowardly attack by drill instructor Sgt. William E. It was a rude awaken growing up black in Alabama and shortly afterwards finding "myself" in a place barely eighteen, and not fighting the Vietnamese, but Tom Metzger and his Ku Klux Klan group.

Tom Metzger (KKK)

As I go by my day planting seeds in my garden or cooking pancakes in my kitchen, there's a dark place in my memory which I was force to re-live on January 6, 2021, because I lived that day July 4, 1973, in Oceanside, California when Tom Metzger KKK finally got their race war between Black and White Marines. There had been constant fighting up on Jackrabbit Hill on Camp Pendleton and a prior assault on me by Sgt. William E. Gugle prior to going to Jackrabbit Hill where I was left to die. I remember a Klansmen telling me I could not come in the NCO club on Jackrabbit Hill and told me, "Do you know what NCO stands for?' I said, "Yes I do" he said, "No Colors Allowed" I said, "I didn't know Allowed" was spelled with a O." Me and a couple other Black Marines vandalize that club because it was their place of meeting to attack us every chance they got. I thought my battle was going to be in Viet Nam but it was all on Jackrabbit Hill.

Metzger had more Klan members up on 33 area than the U.S. Marine Corps had Marines in this white man's Corps, where I was on Request Mast since my arrival to the hill, trying to get black Marines equal rank promotions to white Marines. Metzger recruited from his Fallbrook home right outside the base on Camp Pendleton. It was a Marine Corps where I was never enough. I was only liked when I played football for the Corps, then thrown back in the Brig for Civil Disobedience, now known as "good trouble" for being on Request Mast, after asking the Corps to be compensated the same as white Marines.

Life was hard enough. I did not need to go up to 33 area with a head injury and a lot of personal rage. Sgt. Gugle left me in that pit bleeding from my nose, ear, and head, and was afraid to send me to the hospital for help, the same way he let another Marine drown in a pool. They can't hide the records for platoon 2115, 1973.

After that assault, there was no way for me to be a good Marine. I felt disappointment and confusion, and a lot of anger and rage. My hatred for the Marines and revenge on Sgt. William E. Gugle grew every day because I was injured, confused, and surrounded by black Marines returning home from Vietnam, angry about how they were treated in Nam.

Vietnamese used to tell them, "Go home, black man. This is not your war. Your war is back home in America." They left one war and returned home to another war on Jackrabbit Hill and 33area, where Metzger had signed a lot of the white Marines into the Ku Klux Klan up on Jackrabbit Hill.

I really don't care about reparations under HR40. My reparations are the Marine Corps returning what they took from me, my honorable discharge, and all benefits under that discharge, which I could not defend due to my injuries. I was taken from the Brig on the last leg of my Request Mast, where I was seen by a one-star general who told me I was lucky to be in the Corps and not hanging from a tree in Alabama. I have had the twisties (PTSD) for over 50 years now, which does not include all the discrimination I saw growing up in Alabama, which I was able to overcome. I knew as early as 14 when I was pointed out as the only black in my 9th-grade history class as having a problem being black in a class of all-white boys. I overcame discrimination at a much younger age than that. but it was made personal at that point in life and made more personal at the age of around 17 when I entered the Marine Corps boot camp at MCRD and was assaulted by DI William E. Gugle and left for dead in a pit. Sometimes you can overcome the twisties if you are strong enough to forget all the bad things that you experience for just being black, but then you have reminders that keep bringing it home. Being black is a never-ending story, it seems. My service in the Corps was "good trouble."

References

Civilwar.org

Democracynow.org

Documenting the American South

Josephites.org

Lee, William M.

Los Angeles Times

Moore, Michael

Notre Dame's Study

Samuel John, Darren

Tuskegee Institute Study

Washingtonpost.com

wikipedia.org

Gentry, Bobbi

Carruth, Gorton

Washington Post

Seattle Times

A Private Life: Growing Up Black in America, Chase Hayes

 Growing Up Black in America

Don't get me wrong here, I've had an amazing life. The last thing I want anyone to think is that this book, A Private Life, is about sour grapes. I consider myself a true American red-blooded capitalist like all other good Americans. This book is about my experiences growing up, my experiences fighting back, and growing up to become the best I can be.

Growing up black in the south, I felt that I had the cards stacked against me from the start, despite the fact I managed to get an education, join the United States Marine Corps, and start a successful company. I'm not afraid of hard work, either. I paid for tuition by picking up trash after school, delivered papers before school, and then worked in a shipyard. I owned a boutique, and ran and built a successful company from the ground up with my own blood, sweat, and tears.

There are a million different ways my life could have turned out, but I wouldn't change it for anything. This is my story, my Private Life. I hope you enjoyed reading my story as much as I enjoyed living it.

Red-Headed Book Lover Blog, By Aimee Ann

Memoirs are quickly becoming my favorite books to read, and this thought is enforced thanks to incredible, inspiring books such as this one: A Private Life: Growing Up Black in America. I read a lot of memoirs. Hell, I read a lot in general, but occasionally I will come across a book that strikes a chord with me. The story within the pages of this book, courtesy of the inspirational Chase Hayes, is impeccable, and one that I will not forget for a long time, thanks to its gripping and captivating nature.

A Private Life: Growing Up Black in America is just what the title suggests. It's about a black man growing up in America. However, there is much more to this story than what appears on the surface. It is a gripping, enlightening tale about one man's courageous journey to make something of himself. Chase Hayes, the author of this book, is an incredible man for what he has achieved so far in his life. His story begins with him growing up in the south of America and feeling as if the "cards (were) stacked up against (him)." Despite Chase feeling this way, he managed to overcome the tribulations and prejudices he faced as a young man and was able to get an education, as well as join the United States Marine Corps. Chase, however, wanted more, and soon he built a company from scratch, which turned out to be successful as well as profitable. Chase is a man who is not afraid to get his hands dirty and to work hard for what he wants in life, and these are two qualities everybody should aspire to and try to have.

Chase Hayes's story is one that is incredibly inspiring; I adored how he poignantly and openly described his upbringing and how he felt being a black man growing up in America. It takes a lot for a person to write such things…to bare their soul to readers he does not personally know, so for this, I thank him for sharing his story and for being so open. There should be more people like this. The story of A Private Life is not only compelling as it raises people's awareness to some real issues in this world; it is also an inspirational book because it will inspire you to do better and be better and to finally achieve what you want to in life.

Chase Hayes is not only phenomenal, but also a talented wordsmith. His memoir is beautifully written and flows flawlessly from beginning to end, thanks to his moving literature. I admit, I adored everything about this book, and I also adore the author for how courageous he is. Besides, he is a former Marine! How can somebody not like him?

As I am a huge lover of this book and adore the wisdom and amount of inspiration laced throughout this book, I have no choice but to award this stunning piece of non-fiction a dazzling Five Stars.

Disclaimer

Some names and identifying details have been changed to protect the privacy of individuals. The conversations in the book all come from the author's recollections, though they are not written to represent word-for-word transcripts. Rather, the author has retold them in a way that evokes the feeling and meaning of what was said, and in all instances,the essence of the dialogue is accurate.